INDUSTRIALIZATION and NATIONAL PROSPERITY

(Lessons for the Developing Countries)

LAWRENCE U. EKEH

First published in the UK in 2009

By LUZEK Publishers, London

Email: luzek.publishing@london.com

ISBN 978-0-9563418-0-8 (paperback)

A catalogue record for this book is available from the British Library

Printed and bound in Great Britain by CPI Antony Rowe, Chippenham.

This book is dedicated to
My twin sons
Iyke David Ekeh
And
Ugo Daniel Ekeh,
Who missed out on my fatherly
care while I was writing it

Acknowledgments

The gestation period for this book has been more than 15 years. The conception and development of this knowledge started while I was on a Master's degree programme at the University of Westminster 16 years ago. But the long period has enabled me to gain practical experiences, which are essential for such a unique book.

My experience as a Technology Transfer Consultant took place in both the developed world and the developing world. It is certainly not possible to provide all the answers to all problems of industrialization and national prosperity in any one book. But this experience has equipped me to put reasonable knowledge together for others, in the hope that it can stimulate debate, act as a solution, bring awareness of the constraints facing the developing countries, and above all, that future leaders can be taught the precept of asceticism emphasized in this book.

I therefore acknowledge with gratitude that this book is the fruit of my contact with the intellectuals at the Diplomatic Academy, University of Westminster, London, politicians in the Western and non-Western worlds, and fellow businessmen in both worlds. They are far too numerous to mention here. I owe a debt of gratitude to the staff of Edmonton Central Library, London for the trouble taken to obtain reading materials for me. I am grateful to G. Richard, Sarah Cheeseman, Abukar Osman and Joe M. Kapolyo for their extensive contributions in the final editing, proofreading and preparation of the text.

Without my late grandmother, Ada Ugo, who used to tell me "the world is a marketplace", I may not have seen it that way. Without the late Chibuzo Ajuka, my employer in the early 1980s, who was the architect of many industries in Imo State, my interest in the field would not have been ignited.

Every effort has been made to contact all copyright holders, but if any have been inadvertently omitted, the publishers will be pleased to make the appropriate arrangements at the earliest opportunity.

However, while acknowledging the assistance and support of the above individuals the responsibility for all that is presented in this book lies solely with the author.

Finally, my main wish in writing this book is not only to help the developing countries create more employment opportunities and eradicate poverty, but also to appreciate the efforts being made by some liberal-minded Westerners who also see the world as a global village where all citizens of the world deserve to be treated fairly.

Table of Contents

LIST OF TABLES

LIST OF CASE STUDIES

ABBREVIATIONS

ADB	Asian Development Bank
BOT	Build-Operate-and-Transfer
BTPT	Build-Today-and-Privatize-Tomorrow
DFID	Department for International Development (UK)
DTI	Department of Trade and Industry (UK)
EPZ	Export Processing Zone
FDI	Foreign Direct Investment
GATS	General Agreement on Trade in Services
GATT	General Agreement on Tariffs and Trade
IBRD	International Bank of Reconstruction and Development
IDB	Islamic Development Bank
ILO	International Labour Organization
IMF	International Monetary Fund
IPR	Intellectual Property Rights
JV	Joint Venture
LGS	Loan Guarantee Scheme
MNC	Multinational Corporation
NIE	Newly Industrialized Economy
NTB	Non-Tariff Barriers

ODA	Official Development Assistance
OECD	Organization for Economic Cooperation and Development
PFI	Private Finance Initiative
PPF	Public-Private Finance
RBI	Resource-Based Industries
SAP	Structural Adjustment Programmes
SMI	Small- and Medium-Sized Industries
TNC	Transnational Corporation
TRIMS	Agreement on Trade-Related Investment Measures
TRIPS	Agreement on Trade-Related Aspects of Intellectual Property Rights
UNCTAD	United Nations Conference on Trade and Development
UNCTC	United Nations Centre on Transnational Corporations
UNDP	United Nations Development Programme
UNIDO	United Nations Industrial Development Organization
WIPO	World Intellectual Property Organization
WTO	World Trade Organization

Introduction

While speaking on the Millennium Development Goals, the UN Secretary General Kofi Anan said, "It is the absence of broad-based business activity, not its presence, that condemns much of humanity to suffering". By this he meant that lack of industries and entrepreneurs perpetuates poverty, and poverty cannot be overcome without active engagement of business or industrialization. But how can a nation go about achieving this goal? That is the question this book tries to answer, and in order to plan for the future it is necessary to appreciate how industrialization has evolved over the centuries. The book does not stop at that: it also discusses various issues that may hinder any nation in attaining industrialized status as well as eradicating poverty. I must emphasize that these various issues are the diagnosis rather than the cure, and therefore the book's objective is to provoke thought.

In other words, what the book does not do is prescribe a standard industrial development strategy for all nations of the globe. This is because no single industrial strategy can benefit every country. Strategies which have paid off in one country may be of no relevance in another. For instance, recourse to export-led industrialization may not be an ideal policy for an African country with a large internal market, such as Nigeria. Truly, some of the most successful newly industrialized nations, such as Taiwan, South Korea, Hong Kong and Singapore, have achieved extraordinary industrial growth by using an outward-oriented model driven by market incentives and a strong private sector. But they do not have the same characteristics as Nigeria, South Africa and South American countries.

Most of the Asian Tigers are small in population and in size, and do not have large internal markets. In other words, the book does not advise the developing countries to follow or copy verbatim the pathways adopted by the Asian Tigers or those adopted by the early industrialized nations. It is not a 'cook book' that tells one which ingredient to add in order to blend a certain taste of food. It rather displays, without development or economic jargon, most of the ingredients required, and allows each developing country to make its own choice – a choice of culture and a choice of industrial strategies.

This book starts by excavating the past. This is because in order to understand the present and to be able to predict the future, one has to have an idea of what happened in the past. The truth is always bitter, but do we expose this truth and face the bitterness, or do we continue to pretend that all is well? Obviously, the fight for economic superiority in the past was brutal, crude and wicked; but today, has the world changed? A little, but not entirely, and thanks must go to the liberal-minded Westerners, not the people from developing countries.

Chapter One discusses the early inventions and the struggle of nations to acquire those inventions which were discovered outside their own territories. In the early days there were no intellectual property right laws and the attempts made to acquire those inventions led to wars, plunder and looting. Eventually, the desire to use those foreign goods led to their local production and consequently, created employment locally.

Social virtue is intrinsically linked to the success or failure of industrialization. Chapter Two discusses how as soon as a child is born and opens his eyes, he sees and knows nothing but his nation – the spirit of nationalism. This was the doctrine inculcated in the people of the West by the early philosophers. Where it has its root, the nations tend to industrialize and prosper. It is a culture, and this culture, rather than industrial policies alone, is what enabled the Asian Tigers to grow rapidly. In short, in a country that lacks ascetic virtues – the laying aside of personal interests for the sake of all citizens – the average people in that country will remain poor. This book takes the view that even in countries where such asceticism is lacking, people can still change, for culture is not usually static. Otherwise, the country will wither and die.

Building a more balanced economy will require not only state direction but also the state's ability to choose the right industrial development pathway. Chapter Three uncovers certain obstacles that have hitherto hindered developing countries from industrializing. These are issues that states must look at from a critical perspective. As mentioned previously, experiences of industrialization and each country's problems are so different that using the same approach to solve them all may fail. Two opposing innovative ideas are proposed, as follows: (1) The Multi-Local Enterprises – this approach calls for the pulling together of resources in order to establish a sizeable production capacity; (2) Build-Today-and-Privatize-Tomorrow (BTPT) – this enables the local government, state government and central government to establish industries that may require large capital outlays and privatize them soon after. This is essential because the private businessmen do not have the huge capital to embark on such projects.

In Chapter Four, the lesson is how finance for industrialization can be raised. A case study on how Malaysia raised funds in its quest for industrialized status is used to demonstrate how other developing countries can go about harnessing the same opportunities. The Loan Guarantee Scheme is also an important recommendation for any developing country that is serious about averting poverty and economic disaster. The United Kingdom's experience is used as a case study and is worthy of emulation.

Transfer of technology occurs not only by allowing one nation to acquire physical hardware such as factory machines. It goes beyond that. It involves the transfer of know-how, empowering the recipients of hardware to know the ins and outs of the technology rather than the mere operation of it.

Chapter Five discusses the different types of technology transfer, ranging from foreign direct investment, joint venture and licensing from patents, to turnkey transfer operations. The views of both technology owners and of technology recipients on various issues are revealed, such as control of technology and contributions. The abuses of licences by foreign patent owners, as well as counteractions such as compulsory licences by some developing countries' governments, are also described. On the other hand, there are some opportunities to attract foreign investments, which some developing countries' leaders may not be aware of. This is dealt with in the form of Foreign Investment Guarantee Schemes, which cover multinationals who wish to invest in certain developing countries. Whether these schemes are individually genuine has not been examined in this book. Most of the risks they cover are merely to promote their own export market rather than to transfer technology to developing countries. This book has, however, suggested issues such as enforcing effective laws that may stop multinational organizations from bribing the leaders of developing countries, eradicating agricultural subsidies and reviewing the market liberalization often imposed on developing countries.

Transferring civil technology to developing countries has been an issue since the establishment of GATT in 1948. In theory, even the WTO, which took over from GATT, has accepted the principles of encouraging the transfer of technologies to developing countries. All this has resulted in a number of international instruments and the drawing up of an international code of conduct in transactions relating to the transfer. Whether this will help to bridge the technological gap is yet to be seen, especially as no developing country has ever been to an international court or tribunal for breach of technology transfer laws against any developed country.

An examination of the WTO's understandings or misunderstandings is carried out in Chapter Six. Although the Chinese experience is discussed in Chapter Seven, the intention is not to make comparative references between countries, nor to advise on a particular national model; it is rather to outline a number of strategic options, as well as to highlight the many obstacles hindering developing countries in improving their people's standard of living. How to overcome these obstacles is the puzzle that needs to be solved. The jigsaw will have to be put together in relevant ways, by weighing up and selecting from the workable policies enumerated in this book, by each country's future and current national policymakers.

Finally, the purpose of this book is to provoke thought and to advise developing countries on how to eradicate poverty and improve the lives of their people. But I request sincere support from the developed countries as well as from the leaders of developing countries. This is because people from the rich nations, rich leaders from the developing countries, and people in the poor nations are all citizens of the world. It is therefore fair for equal justice and opportunities through employment creation to apply to all of humanity. Since industrialization is the dynamic instrument used to create employment opportunities and eradicate poverty, the Millennium Development Goals will never be achieved in the absence of broad-based business activities in developing countries.

CHAPTER ONE
Ancient Trade, Inventions and their Diffusion

When the kings took over control of the cities and towns from the Guilds in Europe in the seventeenth century, they formed governments. These governments were made up of representatives of the various cities and towns, with a king as the head. In seventeenth-century England, most of the cities and towns were already wealthy and powerful. The kings were then concerned with transferring to the nation-states they ruled, those principles and practices which had made the cities and towns wealthy and powerful. Having secured political power, governments had to pay attention to economic power. They passed laws and applied economic theories, which they hoped would bring prosperity to their nations.

The laws and theories which the governments in Europe applied in that century, have been classified by historians as the mercantile system. The mercantile system incorporated a number of prevailing economic theories that were applied by the governments of the time in order to achieve wealth and power. All the European governments, including England, Spain, France, Germany and Portugal, wanted to achieve wealth and power, but in the seventeenth century Spain was perhaps the richest and most powerful nation in the world. This was due to the gold and silver that was pouring into Spain from its colonies. Gold and silver were particularly important for countries and individuals at the time. It was gold and silver that enabled the kings to buy the guns they needed to conquer other countries. It was gold and silver that was used to buy timber for the building of ships. It was gold and silver that enabled industrialization to take off.

As a result of the passion for gold and silver worldwide, the yardstick for measuring wealth and power became the volume and amount of gold and silver a country possessed. According to Leo Huberman, in 1757 Joseph Harries wrote in his essay Upon Money and Coins as follows:

Gold and silver, for many reasons, are the fittest metals hitherto known for hoarding: they are durable; convertible without damage into any form; of great value in proportion to their bulk; and being the money of the world, they are the readiest exchange for all things, and what most readily and surely commands all kinds of services (Huberman, 1968).

The importance attached to gold and silver led governments to pass laws forbidding their people from taking these precious metals out of their countries. For example, in 1596 the King of Spain sternly commanded that no gold or silver should be exported from the kingdom. Then, in January 1600 the Pope in Rome decreed that in future, no one should take away from Rome more than five crowns. In short, government after government enacted Act after Act against the export of gold and silver. This was the beginning of international protectionism. But not every country had gold and silver. The question, then, was how could those countries without gold and silver become rich? The mercantilists proposed a "favourable balance of trade" as the way out. This, therefore, brings us to foreign trade.

It was the belief of the mercantilists of the day that for a country to become rich it must engage in international trade. Not only that but it must sell to other countries more than it buys from them in order to maintain a favourable balance of trade. The difference resulting from this favourable balance of trade – the excess of their exports over their imports – would have to be paid to them in gold and silver.

The mercantilists were also very interested in the promotion of industries. They believed that the growth of industries not only meant an increase in exports, which in turn helped to maintain a favourable balance of trade, but it also brought an increase in local employment opportunities. The strategy was to export large volumes of finished goods, importing only what they absolutely needed, and to get the balance in precious metals. The mercantilists also believed that having industries in one's own country meant producing the things people needed locally, rather than buying them from foreign countries.

Then, in the eighteenth century, came the trade wars in Europe – the scramble for overseas markets. The competition for foreign markets among the European countries led rival nations into wars as they fought against each other for colonies. In the course of international exploration and trading, new and better products and technologies made in other countries, particularly India and China, were discovered. As Leo Huberman (1968) explained, "Those Crusaders who returned from their Eastern journey brought back with them an appetite for the strange and luxurious food and clothing they had seen and enjoyed." With the spirit of nationalism and patriotism that prevailed at the time, those newly discovered inventions simply had to be transferred from their countries of origin to Europe. The merchants, who usually travelled with the colonial crusaders, used gold, silver, opium or the use of force to acquire the new technologies. The methods employed in transferring these technologies differed from technology to technology, but before we examine the technology-transfer mechanisms in use today, let us review how some of the ancient inventions were diffused.

Gunpowder

The invention of gunpowder dates back to AD 664, when an Indian monk who went to China identified soils there that contained saltpetre (salt of rock). He demonstrated how a flame was normally emitted whenever such material was put into a fire. The Chinese then investigated this chemistry further, which led to the discovery of the formula for gunpowder. Gunpowder became well known throughout China from then on, but in 1040 some formulas for gunpowder mixtures appeared in a printed book. There were two recipes: one for making explosives and the other for making incendiary weapons. Both involved a high-nitrate powder capable of exploding with sufficient force to propel a missile. The diffusion of gunpowder to the Islamic world, the Mongol Empire and European countries occurred as a result of piracy. Unlike today, there was no intellectual property rights regime to protect the newly invented technologies. Also unlike today, there was no international monitoring body to prevent the transfer of military technology from one nation to another. There was no Coordinating Committee for Multilateral Export Control (Co-Com), no Missile Technology Control Regime (MTCR), no Intellectual Property Rights (IPR), and not even a Restrictive Practices Act.

Although the Mongols conquered parts of China, the Islamic world and Russia, they had no administrative skills to govern or engineering capabilities for construction and technological development. As such, they were unable to govern the territories under their empire. What they did instead was to employ expert technicians from China and administrators from the Arab and Turkish worlds. They also persuaded the Pope to send a hundred trained administrators to help govern the Russian Empire. Unlike later powers, the Mongols encouraged the transfer of technology from one place to another. In the course of the interactions among specialists from different nations, communications about knowledge and techniques occurred; hence, gunpowder technology was widely disseminated. The dialogue in Russia was the basis for the Chinese gunpowder formula passing to the Europeans. The employment of Chinese engineers in Iran (an Islamic country) by the Mongols also indicated that information about gunpowder had passed from China to the Islamic world. Looking at it from another angle, however, the European and Islamic worlds had a level of technological development on a par with China. This is because technology, like water, flows from high ground to low ground, but when the difference in levels is too great it tends to pass through without stopping. The European and Islamic worlds had the skills to copy, modify and adapt the gunpowder technology, and even to develop it into cannon weapons and rockets. The only known official transfer of gunpowder technology from China was to Korea. This occurred when the Japanese ships started to attack Korea. The Koreans asked the Chinese government for help – that is, to allow them to acquire weapons in China. Initially, the Chinese were reluctant, but when Japanese ships started attacking them too, they supplied gunpowder materials and allowed a Chinese technician to go to Korea to instruct the Koreans on how to make gunpowder.

Iron and Steel

In ancient times, the basic process of iron (and steel) manufacture involved smelting and forging. The smelting process involved the heating of iron ore in a furnace using limestone and charcoal in order to get rid of any impurities in the ore. Bellows were used to pump a blast of hot air into the furnace to melt the iron. Then, the iron was poured into moulds of different shapes in order to produce cast iron goods. The forging was done by reheating the pig iron in the furnace and repeatedly hammering the molten iron into different shapes, which removed the impurities. The original invention of this method has not been recorded, but this practice was common in many different parts of the world at the same time. It has not been possible to determine if there was a "transfer of technology" in its diffusion or if the iron products stimulated inventors elsewhere to devise similar ways of achieving the same result. As early as the fifth century BC, iron was smelted in northern Nigeria, although J. M. Roberts was of the view that iron first came to Africa from Asia through Egypt (Roberts, 1944). However, in around 500 BC, iron was already in use in China.

The earliest records about the quantity of iron produced in a country date back to AD 998, when Chinese tax officials calculated the total output that year to be 32,500 tons. But by 1078 Chinese iron production had risen to 125,000 tons a year. The Chinese initially produced iron for agricultural tools, but later shifted production mainly to manufacture military equipment. The main military equipment they produced then (besides gunpowder) was crossbows and arrows. Thousands of these products were made every year. In fact, they were turning out about 16 million iron arrowheads each year. In addition to using iron for arms, the Chinese used cast iron in many consumer products as well as farm tools, and in the building of Buddhist temples. As Pacey explains in his work entitled Technology in World Civilization, "In 1100, China was undoubtedly the most technically advanced region in the world, particularly with regard to the use of coke in iron smelting, canal transport and farm implements" (Pacey, 2001). But despite the military equipment produced, in 1125 a group of nomadic warriors (the Mongols) took over the northern China and Song territories, and as a result, the ironworks were disrupted. Due to this and other subsequent disruptions, the production of iron in China was greatly reduced in 1700. Published figures showed that in 1750 China produced 200,000 tons, while in Europe levels of production were about the same. Yet, there seemed to be no transfer of iron and steel technology between China and Europe. On the other hand, J. M. Roberts, in his Illustrated History of the World, opines that,

"In the thirteenth century, more than a thousand years after the Chinese, Europeans at last learnt how to cast iron by pouring its molten form into moulds. Yet the progress they achieved was won not by inventing things quite anew, but by adopting known methods."

In 1709 Abraham Darby, an Englishman, discovered that coke-fired blast furnaces could be used, thus burning coke as fuel instead of charcoal. He began producing cheaper pig iron using this technique. His discovery, according to Pacey, was entirely independent of the Chinese techniques of the past. Darby had no prior knowledge of the Chinese press. The introduction of this coke-fired iron-smelting technique by Darby at Coalbrookdale, Shropshire in England, was an important milestone; hence, the city remains known as the birthplace of the Industrial Revolution. Darby also smelted large quantities of iron ore. Coke as a fuel was perfect in several respects. Coke was stronger than charcoal, and was often found near deposits of iron ore, saving transportation costs. Like most inventors, Darby did not want to transfer his technology even to his fellow local ironmasters, preferring to reap the benefits alone.

By 1743 Coalbrookdale was made a major centre in ironworks. During the life of Abraham Darby 11 (1750–1791), the family tradition continued and the Coalbrookdale ironworks made the first iron rails in 1767, and from 1777 to 1781 built iron bridges all across England. From then on, iron became the key material for building and making machinery and steam engines. Initially, the steam engine cylinder was made of bronze, and then brass, but in 1718 a steam engine cylinder was made at Coalbrookdale using cast iron. From 1731 onwards, the casting of iron engine cylinders became a routine and major part of the production at Coalbrookdale. By 1796 iron beams had been used in the main structure of a factory building in England, and in 1800 they were used for frames, shafts and wheels in machines. But this is not to say that the first person to invent iron and steel in Europe was Abraham Darby, because by the year 1500, Europe was already producing about 60,000 tons of iron and steel per year. While other ironmasters were using charcoal as fuel, however, Darby was using coke. His discovery showed that a strong blast of hot air could raise the temperature in a coke-fired furnace high enough to melt large quantities of iron ore. It took five days to burn and three days to cool down.

The industry was transformed by 1788: for every ton smelted with charcoal, five tons were being produced with coke. But by 1740 Benjamin Huntsman, also an Englishman, developed a steelmaking process which involved melting the metal produced by the ironmasters. This method also burned off impurities and turned the iron into high quality steel. John Wilkinson used the Boulton-Watt steam engine to power the bellows that blasted air through his iron furnaces, and he built the first iron ships in 1787. Wilkinson was fondly known as "Iron-mad Wilkinson" because of his obsession with iron and its products. He even built a Methodist chapel from iron and stipulated that he was to be buried in an iron coffin.

Despite this progress, European countries were still lagging behind Turkey, Iran, Iraq and Syria in the qualities of the steel they produced. As Anrol Pacey, in his Technology in World Civilization, stated,

"Until a metallurgist named P. A. Anossoff studied steelmaking in Iran in the 1820s and began to manufacture steel of similar quality at a Russian Ironworks, European technologists were completely baffled by the high quality of Turkish musket barrels, Damascus swords and Indian wootz steel. Nothing comparable could be made by any of the Western countries."

But iron was used to make railways, bridges, machinery, steam engines and cutlery, as well as in shipbuilding, building materials and more. In fact, as the rate of railway construction accelerated, unimaginable quantities of iron and steel were required for the rails and locomotives. Notwithstanding these, industrialization cannot start anywhere without a sufficient iron and steel base. Although Europeans were lagging behind, they were mechanically minded people. They were able to learn from other sources such as a compilation of extracts from Arabic, Indian and Chinese authors. Also, with the 'cook book' from Baghdad, new food-processing technologies were invented. Writing on textile processing, Pacey said,

"Suffice it to say that if we see the use of non-human energy as crucial to technological development, Europe in 1150 was the equal of the Islamic and Chinese civilization. In terms of the sophistication of individual machines, however, notably for textile processing, and in terms of the broad scope of its technology, Europe was still a backward region, which stood to benefit much from its contacts with Islam" (Pacey, 2001).

Although Africa had no history of mechanical inventions, some industrial activities such as gold-mining, metalworking, bronze-casting and sculpturing were taking place in many parts of the continent by the time the Europeans came into contact with them. There were bronze-founders, blacksmiths and coppersmiths, and these were early African inventions rather than transferred technologies. In fact, ancient civilizations existed in some African countries before their contact with the outside world, and technologies appropriate to their level of development existed. The ancient metalwork from these civilizations could be found in Egypt, Benin City in Nigeria and other African countries. As W. Rodney in his How Europe Underdeveloped Africa pointed out,

"At the first contact of Europeans with Africans in the 15th century, they had comparable levels of development, though the Europeans had a slight edge".

This slight edge was widened and continued to widen because of the interaction and exchange of information and ideas among the European artisans and merchants.

In any event, by the third century AD, blacksmiths at Nok, a thriving civilization in Nigeria, were smelting and working the metal, and within a few centuries the technology had become widespread throughout much of West Africa. By AD 1000, Nok and other societies had improved the iron technology and were using it for hunting and farming. Obviously, this was

11

an independent innovation, as there was no sign of foreigners at the time, and no recorded technology dialogue within the continent. But unlike in the case of Europe, there was no organized effort in Africa to copy inventions from other parts of the globe.

Gold and Silver

For a very long time, much of the gold used in both the Islamic world and Europe came from Africa. The Portuguese, who discovered the continent, were taking gold out by using caravans of camels to cross the Sahara Desert. From the beginning, the Portuguese and Arab merchants wanted to know the source of the gold, but the Africans did not want them to and successfully kept them in the dark for some time. However, by 1500 the Portuguese were able to discover the mining locations of the gold, which were about 15 metres deep within shafts that were connected to each other. The miners worked in difficult conditions and used iron tools that were not good enough to facilitate the operation. Instead of introducing technology such as water-powered mills for crushing the ore, the Portuguese sent in more labourers from the African coastal regions. This was contrary to the European practice in Mexico and Peru. The transfer of European technology to Mexico and Peru helped in the expansion of silver production there, and a typical example was the extraction of silver from low-grade ore by its amalgamation with mercury. It was called the lead liquation technique and could have been relevant to the mining of gold in Africa. The same liquation process was employed in Germany, where the ores of copper, silver and lead were often found together. About a century before the discovery of gold in Africa, the liquation technique was used to smelt lead away from silver, which contributed greatly to the expansion of mines in Germany. In fact, in Africa, the Portuguese employed only women to wash the gravel from the mines in order to separate it from the gold. What about draining the water from the tunnels? The tunnels were about a metre high in some places and during the wet season they were flooded, and the miners would not work until the dry season arrived. A simple transfer of technology would have been to pump water out of the tunnels using the water-powered engine which had been invented previously. By 1712, when the Newcomen steam engine (used mainly for pumping water from mines) was invented, the Europeans were still digging gold in Africa but did not transfer this technology. The Portuguese also found gold in Zimbabwe, but did not use the technology. Some shafts were up to 25 metres deep, yet they did not transfer any technology to the mining operation in that country.

Books and Paper-Making

To discover when paper was first used as a material on which to write, one would have to go as far back as AD 100, when the Chinese used to inscribe essential documents on stone tablets to ensure their permanence. Whenever they needed extra copies, rather than re-writing they would place paper on the inscribed stone and rub over it with ink. This system helped them to make an accurate copy of the document. Around the same time, instead of stone tablets, carvings were made on wooden blocks, which were placed face upwards on tables. Leaves were then placed on these wooden blocks and ink poured on them and brushed gently. Good copies were produced by using this technique, and this is how printing on paper started. As of AD 671, the same technique was used to print the Buddha's image on silk or paper in China, and the Chinese monk who went to India reported the printing developments in China; hence, the Indians started printing patterns on cloth from carved wooden blocks. In China, the carving of whole pages of writing on wood and printing continued, and developed into book production. By the eleventh century, printed materials had already become the main means of spreading technical information within China.

Paper-like materials were first made of mulberry bark, and then produced from the same vegetable fibre as linen cloth; they had to be pounded in water until a pulp was formed. This technique was first used as early as 200 BC in China, but in AD 100 the real manufacture of paper started. The transfer of this technique reached India via the Buddhist monks in around AD 671; it reached the Europeans via Spain. Spain, being the centre of Islamic scholarship, received it through the Islamic world, of which it was a key member. The knowledge of this technique entered the Islamic world after a battle between the Chinese army and an Arab-led force. The Chinese prisoners of war who had acquired the skill of paper-making were allowed to set up a workshop in Spain, and from there the technique was transferred to other parts of Europe after the conquest of the Islamic world in Spain in 1085 by Christian Europe.

Printing is one of the four great inventions of ancient China. It has a long history and has had a far-reaching impact. Along with the development of hand-carving techniques and the invention of paper-making, people invented printing in practice. With a development process spanning over 5,000 years, printing is a key component of Chinese civilization.

After the invention of printing, it was gradually taken to other countries, giving a great boost to human civilization and social progress. In 1450, influenced by Chinese movable-type printing, Johannes Gutenberg of Germany made movable letters with compound metal types.

In Table 1, the dates refer to when paper was used for writing. According to Pacey, paper-like fabrics, made from mulberry bark, were also used to manufacture clothing and as wrapping material in China, Southeast Asia and the Pacific Islands. In this form, paper may have originated as early as 200 BC in China.

Table 1: The Diffusion of Paper-Making

Place manufacture of paper began	Date when waterwheels began driving the pulping process	First report	Comment
CHINA	AD 100		
TIBET	AD 650		
INDIA			
Buddhists	AD 670		Possibly paper imported from Tibet
Delhi Sultanate	After 1258		
Bengal	1406		
CENTRAL ASIA			
Samarkand	AD 751	AD 1041	Chinese workmen in AD 751

OTHER ISLAMIC COUNTRIES			
Baghdad	AD 794	AD c.950	Probably Chinese workmen at first
Cairo	AD 850		
Damascus	c._1000	c._1000	Existence of paper-mills known but dates uncertain
Tripoli	c._1000		
Sicily	c._1000		
Fez (Morocco)	c. 1050		
Jativa (near Valencia, Spain	1151	1151	Jativa was under Christian rule from c.1238
EUROPE			
Spain			Under Islamic control
Sicily			Under Islamic control
Fariana, Italy		1276	
France, near Ambert	1326	1326	
Nuremberg, Germany	1390	1390	
England	c._1490	1490	

Source: Pacey, 2001: 42

Shipbuilding

Just as the Mongols depended on outside administrators and Chinese engineers to rule their empire and manage their technological inventions, the Europeans depended partly on the Filipino and Indian shipbuilders to upgrade and pilot their ships. First, Vasco da Gama learned new navigational methods and acquired several instruments from his Arab navigator, who was known as Ahmad Ibn Majid. Majid piloted him from the East African coast to South India. It has also been established that collecting information from whoever might disseminate or transfer technology was a Portuguese tradition dating back to the time of Prince Henry the Navigator. Apart from collecting information from China, India and the Islamic world, the Portuguese mariners also collected information from Arab merchants and Jewish cartographers. There was also the transfer of technology from Filipino shipwrights to Spanish designers on local timbers and methods of making dowelled connections between planks. The European ships were built from oak planks, but these could not last because they were always being attacked by woodworm. At that time, the Indians were using teak planks, which lasted much longer; they were also treating the planks with lime to make them resistant to woodworm. This led the Europeans to copy this idea and they started using teak planks in building their own ships. On the other hand, the Indian ships were not built using iron nails but, when they noticed that both the Chinese and European ships were built with nails (and that iron nails not only made strong connections between external planking and frames or bulkheads possible, but they also made the ships less fragile when hit by cannonballs), they also copied this and started using nails in building their own ships. This copying from one nation to another did not infringe any intellectual property or patent laws. Also, one would notice that there must have been an organized cadre of technocrats in each nation – men who were prepared to do the copying in the interest of their people and possibly for personal gain as well.

European development of the steam engine came long after the international transfer of ship technology ideas from one continent to another. Between 1782 and 1784 the patenting of technologies started to emerge in some countries. Consequently, steam engines were used in the shipyards to build gunboats as well as to power factory machines. In 1824–1825 the British realized that gunboats or steamers had the potential in warfare to manoeuvre swiftly and attack enemy ships by catching them unawares. They used them successfully in the "Opium Wars" with China.

16

Several steamers were used, and the operation was led by a steamboat called Nemesis. The success also stimulated Indian shipbuilders to make detailed studies of the steam engine boat. All this dialogue resulted in the transfer of technologies from Europe to Asia and vice versa.

Who Annexed the Planet?

The question now is, despite the early inventions in China, India and the Islamic world, how did the Europeans become number one in technological development? The full answer to this question could form another work of this nature and is therefore beyond the scope of this book. However, we can rephrase the question to ask, why didn't China, India or the Islamic world become number one in the technological race for industrialization?

Before the Europeans came to China, China had money, banking, merchants, markets, entrepreneurial skills, governmental institutions playing developmental roles, etc. but they showed no signs of any pressures to form a more complex economic structure. Also, with their vast internal markets and relative ease of transportation over much of their territory by river, the Chinese merchants had no interest in venturing abroad in search of trade. The Mongols, on the other hand, had different ideas. The Mongols went and conquered Northern China and ruled there for a long time.

When the Europeans started to draw the Chinese into the world economy, the Europeans needed things with which to purchase or exchange for Chinese goods. They used gold, silver and particularly opium to pay for Chinese tea, silks and new technologies. The Europeans promoted the production of opium from poppies grown in India for the purpose of buying Chinese products. The Chinese authorities were alarmed at the scale of drug trafficking in their country and one official wrote to Queen Victoria in England, as follows: "We have heard that in your honourable country, the people are not permitted to inhale the drug. If it is so regarded as deleterious, how can seeking profit by exposing others to its malefic powers be reconciled with the decrees of Heaven?" But the Queen saw the issue as one in which trade was more important than any moral objective, and sent a ship which was fully loaded with opium and arms to China. That led to the first Opium War, which took place between 1840 and 1842.

At the end of the war, Britain imposed an indemnity on China and acquired Hong Kong as a base for trade. In 1857 the Anglo-French forces launched a second Opium War. As a result of their victory, the opium trade was legalized in China, and as a result of the Treaty of Tientsin, both Britain and France imposed more stringent terms on the people of China. More ports were opened for European trade and there were further transfers of technologies from China to Europe. The treaty brought China into the world market, but in a subordinate position. In the case of the Islamic world, following their conquest of Toledo in Spain (which was the Islamic base of invention and studies), the Europeans took all of their inventions, records and some of the experts employed by them, and from then on the Europeans started to consolidate their technological superiority. According to Pacey, Toledo was an important Islamic centre of learning and the place where Christian Europe gained access to Islamic technical books, information about Indian medicine, Hindu numerals, astronomical instruments and Arabic versions of the lost Greek mathematical works (Pacey, 2001).

The Crusaders

It all started in 1009, when the Muslim emperor, known as al-Hakim Bi-Amr Allah of Cairo, sacked the pilgrimage hospice in Jerusalem and destroyed the Church of the Holy Sepulchre. Although his successor permitted the Byzantine emperor to rebuild it, its destruction did not go down well in Europe. In 1063 Pope Alexander XI gave his papal blessing to Iberian Christians in their war against the Muslims, granting both a papal standard (the vexillum sancti petri) and an indulgence to those who were killed in battle. But the turning point in Western European attitude towards the Muslim East came with the Muslim advances in 1071, when at the Battle of Manzikert they defeated the Christian Byzantine Empire that had rebuilt the destroyed Church of the Holy Sepulchre. Contrasting this with the views held by the Muslims, the latter claimed that the Holy Land went back to the Arab conquest of Palestine in the seventh century, and their occupation did not interfere with pilgrimages to Christian holy sites or the security of the monasteries and Christian communities in the area.

On the contrary, the Byzantine Empire ruling from Constantinople, whose emperor at the time was Alexius Comnenus, stated that to the East, the Turks were rapidly encroaching on the empire and had begun attacking pilgrims on their way to – and in – Jerusalem, causing the emperor great distress. He wrote to his friend Robert, the Count of Flanders, in 1093, telling him about the atrocities being committed by the Muslim Turks on the Christian pilgrims, and Robert passed this letter on to Pope Urban XI. The Emperor also appealed to Pope Urban XI for mercenaries to help him resist Muslim advances into the territory of the Byzantine Empire. At this time the Pope was having problems in Europe and had just expanded "The Truce of God", which outlawed fighting from Sunday to Wednesday and banned all fighting involving priests, monks, women, labourers and merchants on any day of the week. This was the Pope's reaction to contemporary French fighting – brothers killing brothers over small pieces of real estate. Meanwhile, in Italy what existed was a collection of city-states constantly being overrun by invading hordes, the most recent being the Normans. The Pope saw this external fighting as a perfect way to solve some of his own local problems, and personally promoted a holy crusade to reclaim the Holy Land from the barbarian Turks.

At the Council of Clermont he called for a large invasion force not only to defeat the Muslims but also to reclaim the Holy Land (where, according to Christian belief, Jesus died, was resurrected and ascended to heaven). According to Fulcher of Chartres, who was at the Council of Clermont where the Pope preached an impassioned sermon to take back the Holy Land, the Pope said:

"Let those who have formerly been accustomed to contend wickedly in private warfare against the faithful fight against the infidel. Let those who have hitherto been robbers now become soldiers. Let those who have formerly contended against their brothers and relatives now fight against the barbarians as they ought. Let those who have formerly been mercenaries on low wages now gain eternal rewards."

As a result, the first crusade was formed in 1095. It consisted of members from France, Italy and England. The term 'crusades' is the name given to the series of military campaigns by Western Christendom to recapture the Holy Land from its Islamic rulers. The crusaders' expeditions took place from 1095 to 1281 and usually got approval from the Pope in the name of Christendom. Crusaders were called Soldiers of the Church. A crusader would pronounce a solemn vow and then receive a cross from the Pope or his legates.

Prior to the launching of the crusades, however, there were large groups of armed warriors in Western Europe who were fighting among themselves, such as the Vikings, Slavs and Magyars. Thirty years earlier,

William the Conqueror had united England under one crown. The Church at that time had tried to stem the violence with Peace and Truce of God movements, and was successful to some extent. But when the Pope launched military campaigns, using the crusades against pagans and Muslims to the East, those trained warriors, having abandoned their internal fighting and become Christians, joined the crusades, grabbed the opportunity to go for territorial expansion and started to unleash their violence and killing skills. As a result, they became the most striking expression of the new temper and outlook of European Christians. Many of them had no respectable motives and were there to loot booty and grab lands. This, no doubt, became the first instance of European overseas imperialism, as the area in question is now called Israel, and also includes parts of Lebanon and a small stretch of Syria and south-eastern Turkey. It was a small stretch of land, rich in religious heritage and holding the promise of bestowing riches upon the men who could control the "land flowing with milk and honey".

Initially, the Catholic Western Church was genuine and honest, but when it realized that the greater the area of Christendom was the greater the power and wealth of the Church would be, it extended its objectives beyond regaining the Holy Land and converting nations to Christianity, to economic and political reasons and for the benefit of all the European merchants who supported them. This is how Leo Huberman (1968) explained it:

From the point of view of religion, the results of the Crusades were short-lived, since the Moslems eventually took back the kingdom of Jerusalem. From the point of view of trade, however, the results of the Crusades were tremendously important.

He further wrote that the crusades helped to wake up Western Europe from its feudal slumber by spreading prayers, fighters, workers, and a growing class of merchants all over the continent. Roberts has described it thus:

"The Crusades had changed the outlook of Christians, too. The new militancy and determination they showed to go out and conquer in the name of the Cross was to be one psychological root of the confidence with which later Europeans went out and took the world (Roberts, 1994)".

Huberman went further and gave an example of how six ambassadors went to the Doge of Venice to ask for help in transporting the crusaders during the Fourth Crusade, which began in about 1202. One of the men was Ambassador Villehardouin, who addressed the Doge as follows:

'Sire, we have come to you on behalf of the noble barons of France who have taken the cross ... they pray to you, for God's sake ... to endeavour to furnish them transports and ships of war.'
'Under what conditions?' asked the Doge.
'Under any conditions that you may propose or advise, if they are able to fulfill them,' replied the messengers ...
'We will furnish huissiers [vessels having a door (huis) in the stern which could be opened so as to take on the horses] for carrying 4,500 horses and 9,000 esquires, and vessels for 4,500 knights and 20,000 foot-soldiers. The agreement shall be to furnish food for nine months for all these horses and men. That is the least we will do, on condition that we are paid four marks per horse and two marks per man ... And we will do more still: we will add fifty armed galleys, for the love of God, on the condition that as long as our alliance shall last ... we shall have one half and you the other,' responded the Doge ...
The ambassadors said, 'Sire, we are ready to make this agreement.'
    (Huberman, 1968)

Of course, the Doge of Venice was willing to help the crusaders 'for the love of God', but the real motive was the profit/booty incentive. At this stage, the crusaders, nobles and knights who wanted booty were no longer getting the Pope's consent. The merchants who went with them were buying and stealing new products and technologies from other nations, unbundling them, copying and sometimes modifying them to suit the European environment. This helped the Europeans to stabilize their technological superiority, and from then on, these expeditions to the Eastern Mediterranean gave the Europeans extensive experience with fortifications and incendiary weapons, with which they went and conquered the rest of the world.

Table 2: The Crusaders' Movement

1095 AD	Pope Urban XI proclaims the First Crusade at the Council of Clermont.
1099	The capture of Jerusalem and foundation of the Latin kingdoms.
1144	The Seljuk Turks capture the (Christian) city of Edessa, whose fall inspires St Bernard's preaching of a new crusade (1146).
1147/9	The Second Crusade, a failure (its only significant outcome was the capture of Lisbon by an English fleet and its transfer to the King of Portugal).
1187	Saladin re-conquers Jerusalem for Islam.
1189	Launching of the Third Crusade, which fails to recover Jerusalem.
1192	Saladin allows pilgrims access to the Holy Sepulchre.
1202	The Fourth Crusade, the last of the major crusades, which culminates in the capture and sacking of Constantinople by the crusaders (1204), and the establishment of a Latin Empire.
1212	The Children's Crusade.
1216	The Fifth Crusade captures Damietta in Egypt, but is lost soon after.
1228/9	Emperor Frederick XI (excommunicated) undertakes a crusade and recaptures Jerusalem, and crowns himself King.
1239/40	Crusades by Theobald of Champagne and Richard of Cornwall.
1244	Jerusalem retaken for Islam.
1248/54	Louis IX of France leads crusade to Egypt where he is taken prisoner, ransomed, and goes on a pilgrimage to Jerusalem.
1270	Louis IX's second crusade against Tunis, where he dies.
1281	Acre, the last Frankish foothold in the Levant, falls to Islam.

Source: Roberts, 1994: 266

The first four crusades were the most important and this period was known as the crusading era. A number of crusades were undertaken, but some without the Pope's blessing. Some targeted the non-Christians while others were against the monarchs who had offended the Pope.

Accumulated Capital Came from Early Commerce

An accountant says Total Assets minus Current Liabilities is equal to Owner's Capital. Assuming the business has not started trading, the long-term liabilities might be loans taken plus the initial funds the owner brought into the business. But where did his initial capital come from? Today, the industrialist will save, borrow from banks and relations or sell his property to start industrial production, but in those days, if borrowing, where did the lender get their gold or money? If the industrialist used his savings, where did he get the money or gold he had saved? At the time, there were no properties to sell. In short, how did the Europeans accumulate the money with which they started the Industrial Revolution? Obviously, the capital that was used to start the Industrial Revolution was not generated out of thin air, or by the frugal habits which the Protestants preached. There was also no national resolve to increase the rate of savings for the sake of the new forms of factory organization, which were being preached by the churches that were breaking away from Catholicism. Some writers claim that the increase in output generated by the factories was more than sufficient to pay their capital costs over a short period of time. Fine, but where did the money for the very first factories come from? We have also been told by authorities on the subject that, in those days, capital was accumulated mainly through commerce. Commerce nowadays is mainly the exchange of goods and services, but in those days commerce also included the slave trade, exploitation, technology piracy, conquest and plunder.

John A. Hobson was seen as one of the best authorities on the subject and wrote as follows: "Thus early was laid the foundation of the profitable trade which furnished to Western Europe the accumulations of wealth required for the later development of capitalistic methods of production at home" (Hobson, 1894). Mr Hobson was referring to the Italian commerce with the East Indies in the thirteenth and fourteenth centuries. Another well-known authority on the subject was Karl Marx, who said:

"This discovery of gold and silver in America, the extirpation, enslavement, and entombment in mines of the aboriginal population, the beginning of the conquest and looting of the East Indies, the turning of Africa into a warren for the commercial hunting of black-skins, signalised the rosy down of the era of capitalist production. These idyllic proceedings are the chief moments of primitive accumulation" (Marx, 1867).

The Slave Trade

"To be sold, a Negro boy, aged eleven years. Enquire of the Virginia Coffee-house in Threadneedle Street, behind the Royal Exchange" (London Daily Journal, 1728)

This advert was placed by a merchant called John Norton. It shows how Black Africans were sold as a commodity, even boys of eleven! According to R. S. Reddie (2007), the Negro slave trade was started in the fifteenth century by the Portuguese, and the other 'civilized' Christian European countries followed soon after. The first Englishman who saw it as a lucrative business was John Hawkins. He later became Sir John Hawkins, having been knighted by Queen Elizabeth I for his slave-trade expedition. How did he do it? He went to Africa and deceived the African Christians by telling them that he was taking them on an adventure to see their fellow Christians in London. Innocently, these people trooped into the three waiting ships that headed to England, only to be sold as raw materials for plantation work in the New World. The Queen was so impressed with Sir John's success that she offered to be a partner in his second expedition of 1564, which brought slaves from West Africa and sold them to Spanish colonists in the Caribbean. The Queen loaned Sir John a ship, which was inscribed with the word "JESUS". This trade brought in huge profits and fed the growing supply of capital in Europe. As Leo Huberman (1968) states, "Trade with the colonies brought wealth to the mother country". It built the early fortunes of European merchants. The slave trade was regarded as infamous; yet many respectable merchants in America and Europe grew rich on its profits.

The business was made more organized in 1672 by the Royal African Company. They would purchase from dealers in West Africa and then ship their goods across the Atlantic, where the slaves worked on plantations in the Caribbean and in the colonies of North America. In 1711 another company, called the South Sea Company, was founded – solely to raise money for the British government through the slave trade. The government agreed to pay interest on the capital and granted the new company a monopoly of trade with Central and South America. The coast of North America, which was an area controlled by the Spanish and known as the South Sea, was conceded to Britain in 1713 at the Treaty of Utrecht. As a result of this treaty, the company secured the Asiento Contract to supply 4,800 black slaves to Spanish America every year.

The Royal Africa Company, the South Sea Company and other companies founded by individual merchants, united into a single body acting as a unit with one management. The aim was to overcome the problems of trading in unknown lands, under unfamiliar conditions and with strangers. In addition, the advent of the joint stock company enabled merchants to buy shares and contribute to the capital with which to undertake the vast trading activities. The long and expensive journeys required would involve buying or hiring ships, paying the crew members, and obtaining equipment and food. The cost would have been too much for individual merchants; hence, the joint stock company. The first English joint stock company was called the Merchant Adventurers. There were 240 shareholders who each contributed £25 – a huge sum of money in those days. The slave merchants bought shares in joint stock companies to enable the great trading, pirating expeditions, colonizing expeditions and privateering to take place. In short, whoever had money could become a partner in a joint stock company by purchasing shares. It was a period of commercial revolution. There were seven "East India" companies, four "West India" companies, assorted "Levant" companies and other "African" companies. These joint stock companies made huge profits, and these profits were used to finance industrialization in Europe. A typically high rate of profit was secured in Sir Francis Drake's expedition, where Queen Elizabeth took shares in return for loaning some ships. The profit on this one trip was as huge as 4,700%. Another example was that of Vasco da Gama, whose first voyage to India gave him a profit of 6,000%. That was the Golden Age of commerce, when huge fortunes were made and capital for the seventeenth and eighteenth century industrialization of Europe was accumulated.

The joint stock companies were so powerful that they could do anything in their trading territory and get away with it, just like some present multinational oil companies do. They could pollute/destroy the environment; they could mastermind/instigate the murder of anyone in the host country who opposed their interests; they could overthrow a government that opposed their interests; and they could influence the cultural behaviour of the people, say, by bribing government officials and chiefs in order to get what they wanted or to suppress opposition. Today's multinational companies can often do this and get away with it because they have one thing in common with the joint stock companies of the seventeenth century – both pay duties and taxes to their own governments who, in turn, must protect them. In the seventeenth century, much of the credit for European trade expansion must also go to these joint stock companies, who helped to create a demand for European goods and open up areas with new sources of raw materials.

A particularly interesting source of capital accumulation was the trade in human beings - the black-skinned natives of Africa. This trend continued even in 1788 when there was a petition to the House of Commons by the merchants of Liverpool, that the horrible trade of live human beings was unbecoming to a civilized country. Later, one Professor H. Merivale delivered a series of lectures at Oxford on "Colonization and Colonies". During his lecture on one occasion, he asked two important questions: "What raised Liverpool and Manchester from provincial towns to gigantic cities? What now maintains their ever active industry and their rapid accumulation of wealth?" Just like Marx, the professor condemned the type of commerce that was going on, but that made him unpopular.

However, in 1807, with the help of people like William Wilberforce, John Newton, John Wesley, the founder of the Methodist Church, and others, the parliament in England abolished the slave trade and forbade its ships from participating in it. So, in 1833 the evil trade was abolished throughout the British Empire. Not only did the British government abolish it, the Royal Navy also helped to police the abolition of the slave trade on the high seas by stopping other nations' ships from engaging in it.

However, by that time great damage had been done to the continent of Africa. The growth of such trade had set back cultural, commercial and technological development from the fifteenth to the nineteenth century. The captured people were mainly young men and women who, as in every other country, were potentially more technologically innovative than the old and the children they left behind. Even the ones left behind were running for cover from the human hunters and, as such, the already developed technologies, which had existed before the arrival of the Europeans, were abandoned and forgotten. The slave trade therefore contributed greatly to the backwardness and even the increasing stagnation of technology in Africa.

But there is no doubt that such trade brought in the capital that was needed to start capitalist production in Europe. And, of course, when the slave trade finally ended, the merchants had to put their capital to use somewhere else. They invested the money made from the slave trade into factory production. The Industrial Revolution in Europe was not financed by bankers but rather by such merchants. They were often willing to invest in the new, expanding business enterprises, which were then being stimulated by the advent of factory machinery in the eighteenth century. There were two main modes of investment: (1) they would lend money and receive interest on their loans in exchange for a mortgage on a property (a mode open to the few who had properties). If the borrower failed to repay, they would take over the title of the building; (2) by financing major projects, for example London projects like railways, canals and so forth, the merchants who bought stocks or shares in a company received dividends, that is, a share of the profits. By 1773, the stock trade had expanded so much that a Stock Exchange house had been built, and investors seeking to put money into the new railway companies were rushing to invest in it. The lesson here is that the merchants did not take or invest their money abroad. Rather, they invested in factories and projects in their own countries.

The Italians, the Dutch and the Spanish all accumulated their production capital through such commerce. The inhuman treatment suffered by locals in the colonies at the hands of their Spanish and Dutch masters action was the worst in history. Sir T. S. Raffles, the one-time governor of the Island of Java, described the relationship between Holland and the colonies as "one of the most extraordinary relations of treachery, bribery, massacre, and meanness" (Huberman, 1968). A typical example of Dutch meanness in their quest to accumulate capital can be illustrated by an incident that took place in 1641 – when the Dutch wanted to take over Malacca (a Sri Lankan port) where a Portuguese noble was already the governor. The Dutch promised the Portuguese governor £21,875 as the price of his treasure, but when they were allowed in the Dutch assassinated the Portuguese governor in order to avoid making any such payment to him. "Wherever they set foot, devastation and depopulation followed. Banjuwangi, a province of Java, in 1750 numbered over 80,000 inhabitants, in 1811 only 18,000. Sweet commerce!" said Sir Raffles. He also confirmed that they made huge profits in Java (Huberman, 1968).

Let us look at what a writer in 1838 wrote in the Orient Herald about the British in India:
"Our empire is not an empire of opinion, it is not even an empire of laws; it has been acquired; it is still governed ... by the direct influence of force. No portion of the country has been voluntarily ceded ... we were first permitted to land on the sea coast to sell our wares ... till by degrees sometimes by force and sometimes by fraud ... we have put down the ancient sovereigns of the land, we have stripped the nobles of all their power, and by continual drains on the industry and resources of the people we take from them all their surplus and disposable wealth" (Huberman, 1968: 167).

At this time thousands of native Indians were starving to death. A small matter, then, and so why wouldn't the Europeans continue to accumulate capital for industrial production? This new wealth/profit was saved by its owners, who believed that reinvesting it into factories would yield even greater profits.

Apart from human hunting, other materials used to accumulate industrial capital were gold and silver from places like Africa, Peru, Mexico and India. There were few products from Europe with which to engage the Chinese in the form of trade by barter. Furthermore, the European products were of inferior quality compared to those of China and the Islamic countries. This meant that almost everything they bought from China and India was paid for in gold and silver. Therefore, the Europeans had to discover new sources of gold and silver. But where did the European gold and silver come from? This is how Leo Huberman explains it in his book, Man's Worldly Goods:

Then ask a Mexican or Peruvian Indian to tell you the story of the first contact of his ancestors with the white man in the sixteenth century. The natives were given Christianity – and with it enforced service in the mines, beatings, killings. But what a tremendous store of gold and silver they dug out of the ground to be shipped to the Old World – there to find its way eventually into the hands of the merchants and bankers! (And gold and silver in those hands was not idle; it was used to give credit; it was used either in loans to manufacturers or in trading, to bring in a greater amount of money. In short, it was capital.) (Huberman, 1968)

He further narrated that from 1545 to 1600, it was estimated that each year about two million pounds was repatriated back to Europe from America, and that from 1545 to 1560 the Spanish mint alone increased from

45,000 to 270,000 kilograms, and from 1580 to 1600 the production went up to 340,000 kilograms, or about eight times what it used to be in 1520. Furthermore, in 2001 Arnold Pacey, a physicist-turned-historian, wrote that around AD 1500 the West African region was the source of about half of Europe's supply of gold. These stores of gold from both South America and Africa must have also facilitated the trade and technology transfer from China to Europe, and vice versa.

Why Industrialization?

England has become known as the birthplace of the Industrial Revolution. Therefore, tracing the reason why industrialization took off in England will enable us to answer the question of why any country should attempt to industrialize in the first place. It all started with the invention of one man called James Watt. Mr Watt invented the steam engine in 1776. By 1800 it was in use in 30 collieries, 22 copper mines, 28 foundries, 17 breweries and 84 cotton mills. Although other machines had been invented in England in the past, the steam-powered engine led to an important change in the production system. With the new division of labour which the steam engine entailed, it made the production system faster, leading to increases in output. This led to greater profits for the factory owners, which attracted yet more investors into production. The capital accumulated through the slave trade already existed. The owners of this idle capital saw that they could invest their wealth in the factories and make even more money.

Unlike in the present competitive age, there was no competition whatsoever at the time for the producers of factory goods. Instead, there was both local demand and burgeoning foreign demand for the products being churned out. The huge demand for factory goods meant that all available surplus labour was absorbed in the factories. People enjoyed the consumption of factory goods, their health improved and they lived longer as a result. Not only that, but premature deaths also declined and thus the population increased at a faster rate. For instance, the average population increase in England before 1700 was a steady one million every 100 years. But between 1700 and 1800 the increase in population was three million. This also meant even more demand for factory goods. At the same time, trade by barter was necessary in order to obtain things from the new territories that the Englishmen had discovered. This, too, meant more demand for the factories' outputs for the world at large.

It is obvious that in the capitalist system, production does not take place unless there is hope of making a profit. But for the government, the level at which industrialization was absorbing the surplus labour was very important. In 1865 Friedrich Engels described the unemployed people in England as follows: "The moneyless bellies, the labour which cannot be utilised for profit and therefore cannot buy, is left to the death rate". So, industrial production created jobs for the "moneyless bellies" that would have been left to the "death rate". What about the standards of living? Industrialization is inextricably linked with improved living standards. In a nutshell, the benefits of industrialization can be summarized as follows:

• The empirical evidence indicates that industrialization absorbs surplus labour wherever it takes place;
• With earnings made while working in factories, workers meet their basic needs; hence, poverty is eradicated;
• With reasonable wages for workers, their standard of living is improved;
• Industrialization brings with it essential amenities, including social cohesion;
• Industrial need for agricultural raw materials leads to increased economic activities in the agricultural sector;
• It leads to social transformation;
• It leads to the acquisition of new skills.

But the question is, is industrialization the only way to eradicate poverty and improve a country's standard of living? The answer is yes, because agriculture itself can be "industrialized". It only involves the enlargement of scales of production on estates or plantations, the increased use of machinery and the employment of surplus labour by farmers. In fact, agricultural production is not restricted to food alone. Vegetable fibres, oil seeds, wool and cotton are all industrial raw materials as well as agricultural products. Therefore, this means that an agricultural economy with surplus farmland in Africa may eradicate poverty by exporting food and/or agricultural raw materials to other economies. However, this can only happen if there are no agricultural subsidies within the African region, and provided the African continent is not being used as a dumping place for subsidized agricultural products made elsewhere. It is only then that African farmers may prosper. This is because the increased output and increased incomes in the agricultural economy will lead to the eradication of poverty and improved standards of living. After all, the economic development of Denmark, New Zealand and Australia in the late nineteenth century went through precisely this process. Their economic growth was initially based on the export of dairy products and meat to the industrialized economies of Europe. At this stage, let us look at the views of an early writer like Kitching on development, and review what he had to say on industrialization strategies for each nation:

"Any strategy must take into account factors including the demographic and geographical size of the economy involved, its resource endowment (including its "human capital" endowment) and its role in the world economy at the point at which industrialization is attempted. For small, resource-poor Third World countries, a development sequence which begins with the expansion of primary product exports, moves to the manufacture of simple inputs and basic consumption goods for the primary producers (usually, though not always, peasant producers), and from there to the manufacture of labour-intensive consumer and producer goods for export and domestic consumption, is a particularly more appropriate industrialization strategy for small peripheral economies than either "crash" heavy industrialization under state auspices or luxury "import substitution" industrialization undertaken under the auspices of multinational corporations. Such a strategy is particularly desirable in that it can accommodate forms of rural " agro-industry" which can act as a counterbalance to over-rapid urbanization" (Kitching, 1982, 1989: 192).

From the start of his book, Kitching makes his views clear by saying that "if you want to develop you must industrialize". He has also noted, however, as above, that industrialization should not be based on non-agricultural products alone.

But let us end this chapter by quoting Huberman (1968: 129): "To a group of men who were to set up a plant for the manufacture of silk and of cloth of gold and silver in seventeenth-century France, the government gave many valuable privileges as well as direct aid in money. One of the principal means of attaining this end (common good of our subjects) is the establishment of arts and manufactures, both for the hope which they give of enriching and improving this kingdom, that we may no longer have to go to our neighbours like beggars … seeking afar what we do not ourselves posses, and also because it is an easy and good means of cleansing our kingdom of the vices produced by idleness, and the only way

31

by which we may no longer have to send out of the kingdom gold and silver to enrich our neighbours".

CHAPTER TWO
How Culture Shapes National Prosperity

The Spiral of Culture

In the first chapter the historical facts behind European industrialization were examined. This is because it would be difficult to understand the present without some appreciation of how the present came about and how it differs from the past. The important lesson we have learnt so far is how the Europeans were able to come together, conquer the world and diffuse the technologies they found elsewhere. But the spiral of culture that enabled them to come together is yet to be uncovered. Another important and more recent lesson to learn is whether the industrial policies of the Asian Tigers were responsible for their high rates of growth, or if it was perhaps merely their cultural behaviour. If we accept the hypothesis that industrial policies were responsible for the Asian Tigers' progress, then why were the levels of progress not evenly distributed among the countries that basically adopted the same industrial policy? Put another way, given the same policy, why did some countries fare better than others? The answer is that the capability of each state to implement the industrial policies chosen is where culture becomes relevant. To summarise, the society with long traditions of honest and competent civil servants and politicians progressed more rapidly than those with corrupt civil servants and politicians. The laws of economics are just as valid in the UK, Japan, Nigeria and the United States, or even in Cameroon, but there are significant cultural variations in their applications. What matters is not just the industrial policy per se but also the local culture. No wonder Adam Smith wrote in his work The Theory of Moral Sentiments that economic motivation is highly complex and embedded in social habits and culture. But because of the change in the name of the discipline from "political economy" to "economics" between the eighteenth and late nineteenth centuries, economics seems to have lost its relationship with culture. Taking the discipline back to its original name, one can see how taking account of culture shapes all aspects of economic behaviour.

Cultural factors no doubt shaped and underpinned the prosperity of the European continent. It is therefore only natural that one compares and contrasts different cultures and relates them to their economic performance. An examination of how the enormous prosperity created by cultures that recognize liberal regimes, equal rights and human dignity (at least locally) has shown the way for other societies of the globe. It means that societies can be richer or poorer depending on their cultural norms. Does this therefore mean that the government setting up gigantic projects here and there or getting more annual revenue cannot guarantee a "great society"? Indeed, it cannot. A thriving economy depends on the people's customs, habits, moral obligations and ethics. Industrialization is inextricably connected with customs, habits and ethics. In short, there is no form of economic activity, from running a photo laboratory or dry-cleaning business to manufacturing spare parts, that is not affected by the customs, habits and ethics of the people involved in running and using it.

A broad term that describes the social life of people and covers concepts like customs, habits, moral obligations, norms, rules and ethics, as well as shapes a society, is culture. Before we examine cultures carefully, the first question is, are there some cultural differences that separate the developed countries from the developing countries? Secondly, if the answer is yes, does this imply that all the developed countries have similar cultures? We assume that the answer to this is no. So, what are the common cultural characteristics among them? Can the application of the culture of a developed country lead to creative change in developing countries? What are the cultures that may hinder the economic and social progress of a society? What are the cultural characteristics that can leapfrog a poor economy into a prosperous one? All this suggests that the issues surrounding international competition, economics, politics and poverty can be traced to a society's culture. We shall find the answers to these questions in this chapter.

First of all, let us look at the meaning of "society". Any society is made up of individuals – one definition is a group of individuals forming a single community with its own distinctive culture and institutions. These individuals all behave and perceive right and wrong in almost the same way. But every individual seeks to have his or her own dignity recognized by other individuals. The struggle for this recognition has shifted from oratory performance, skills acquisition, having many wives and children (in some countries), to status and wealth accumulation. Beyond satisfying basic material needs, wealth accumulation is for the sake of social recognition.

Some individuals are interested in accumulating for themselves while others accumulate for their larger families – and ultimately, the entire society. Those accumulating for themselves are either people with low ambitions or less opportunity, or the greedy and selfish individuals – driven by the desire to "better their condition" – while those accumulating for society do so for the sake of humanity or status symbols, and perhaps want to be remembered for their contributions to the common good. For the selfish or self-interested individuals, what do they gain if, after accumulating their wealth (most likely, unfairly), they just die, leaving all the wealth behind? However, the ways and manners of accumulating this wealth or recognition are what shape a society's culture. A society that prides itself on killing people elsewhere in the name of war or holy war will influence its people's attitudes at home. War is supposed to be something of the past, when religions, villages, kings and tribes used to seek recognition by fighting bloody battles with one another for primacy. It has now shifted from military superiority to economic superiority, and from wealth destruction to wealth creation. This is the majority view, and since the majority carries the vote, the minority has no choice but to follow.

As we will discover in this chapter, a society with high mutual levels of trust will be able to establish large-scale industries that are vital for global competitiveness and the economic well-being of its people. On the other hand, in a society with low trust levels, people find it difficult to come together in order to establish and operate competitive large organizations. In the latter types of society only, the state steps in to promote durable and globally competitive firms. This "trust" also takes us to what a sociologist, James Coleman, called "social capital": the ability of people to subordinate their individual interests to those of larger groups or the whole society. He argued that the concept of social capital starts from the premise that capital is embodied less in factories, machines and land. Rather, people's ability to associate with each other is crucial not only to economic life but to virtually every other aspect of social existence. The success of social existence is rooted in the common culture, and culture without trust is a failure because trust has a large and measurable economic value. Francis Fukuyama, in his book Trust, states:

The accumulation of social capital, however, is a complicated and in many ways mysterious cultural process. While governments can enact policies that have the effect of depleting social capital, they have great difficulties understanding how to build it up again.

He is also of the view that there must be reciprocity, moral obligation, duty towards community and trust, which are all based on habit rather than rational calculation. With these thoughts in mind, I will move on to discuss in the rest of this chapter the culture, trust and social capital that are the fundamental bedrock for any country that needs to industrialize and create employment opportunities for its people.

The Spirit of Nationalism

The nineteenth century witnessed the growth of the "nation" ideology. The concept of nation rests on sovereignty, and the ideology originated in medieval times in England. However, it was Rousseau of France who first wrote about the possibility of creating a nation by a process of ideological indoctrination. He wrote that to achieve this, "it is the task of education" to give each human being a national form, and so direct his passion, thought, and tastes towards becoming a patriot to his nation. On first opening his eyes, a child must see his country, and until he dies, must see nothing else" (Howard, 2007). Then came the French Revolution, which led humankind into an era of escalating nationalism, and reached its climax in Europe in 1914–1918. The frenetic nationalism of the time led to the First World War. Also, in Germany in 1806, Fichte proposed a total change in the prevalent patterns of education. He said, "By means of this new education we want to mould the Germans into a corporate body, which shall be stimulated and animated in all its individual members by the same interest" (Fichte, 1806). This therefore meant that if the Germans were to ignite the spirit of nationalism, other members of the world community would follow. As Michael Howard put it, "where the Germans led, others followed" (Howard, 2007). On the other hand, in 1870 Professor John Ruskin told his audience at his Inaugural Lecture as Slade Professor of Fine Arts at Oxford, that it must be the task of England,

"..still unregenerate in race, to found colonies as fast and as far as she is able, formed of her most energetic and worthiest men – seizing every piece of fruitful waste ground she can set her foot on, and there teaching these her colonists that their chief virtue is to be fidelity to their country and that their first aim is to advance the power of England by land and sea" (Huberman, 1968).

Further, Charles Dilke's Greater Britain, which was published in 1867, urged the British to populate the empty spaces of the world with their people and to rise up and educate the inferior races they found there. The point here is not their expansionism or the concept of an empire, but rather that Englishmen were able to become a great imperial power because of their new self-consciousness – their spirit of nationalism. The achievement of nationhood and the creation of independent political entities corresponding to cultural communities and defined by language, became the greatest aspirations of young idealists in nineteenth-century Europe. This evolution of the nation and of nationalism even led to the transformation of societies from agrarian to industrial. Their aspirations became a success in the nineteenth century, when new states started to emerge and some old states tried to consolidate into single ones. Governments were formed, and these governments took power and control of education.

Education was then used to create national awareness, national identity and social cohesion. Using education, all nations tried to inculcate in their citizens the spirit of nationalism in order to preserve their social cohesion and their ideology. A society that is not sure of its ideology is less significant on the international scene. In short, national attitudes, myths, perceptions and beliefs had to be inculcated in the minds of everyone and particularly, in the minds of pupils by their schoolteachers. The education was in English, German and French, and it was the same in America. Before the idealists' proposals in England, Fichte (1806) in Germany went on to say that every nation should wish to spread its own ideas and ways of life as far as it could, and as far as its power would allow it, even to incorporate the whole of mankind. He believed that this was due to a compulsion which God had implanted men with and on which the society of nations, their mutual friction and development rested. But Fichte did not foresee that such an ideology could lead to worldwide struggle: a struggle not just for self-determination but a struggle for power and a struggle to dominate other nations with one's own national culture and ideology, all at the expense of other nations. Again came the process of the natural selection and evolution theory expounded by Charles Darwin (1859):

In the conceptual framework provided by the ideology of nationalism in international relations was the art of surviving in a jungle of predators in order to preserve one's own superior culture and ultimately, to impose it upon inferior adversaries.

This theory was usurped and applied to races and nations by the so-called 'Social Darwinists', who used it to justify European empires in terms of more evolved nations ruling the world as part of the "natural" order of things. But the catastrophe caused by the theory started in Europe. It had to, because there was no single ideology across the whole of Europe; this consequently led to the two world wars. Today, the victors of those wars have set the pattern for the present and future development of humankind. Unfortunately, this development has retained the idea of "nationalism". Nationalism is still being promoted by their methods of teaching history and by various governments' actions. The two world wars have not taught the world enough lessons. For example, when children in schools and universities are taught the nineteenth-century history of wars and conquests, emphasis is placed on the "founding myths" of their own countries. Then, they grow up thinking that they have the divine right to rule others. The brainwashing of people, using education, into thinking that they are superior human beings does not go hand in hand with international peace. It has led the world into a dismal cycle of disruption and oppression, thereby creating rich and poor nations, as if we are still in a Stone Age society where the strong will take everything for themselves, while the weak will be trampled upon until they can no longer rise. This is making it increasingly difficult for a global community to emerge.

Let's face the truth. It is too late to denationalize us all. Without nationalism we would not hear of or talk about the British economy, German economy, French economy, American economy or Chinese economy. Without nationalism, the jobs of presidents, prime ministers and their fellow politicians are gone. Without these people, would the world actually be a safer place? Without "nationalism", might the world be a better place? I doubt it! In Japan, for example, there is a business network known as the keiretsu. Members of the keiretsu buy from one another rather than from a foreign company that might offer better quality and a better price. And, according to Fukuyama (1995), when a Japanese executive goes to work, he toils not just for himself, his family and his company, but also, and perhaps more importantly, for the greater glory of the Japanese nation. It is the spirit of nationalism that makes most soldiers sacrifice their lives for their nations. Another example is in the case of Germany. During the oil crisis of the early 1970s, the German car-makers Daimler-Benz (the makers of Mercedes Benz) suffered a great decline in sales and nearly went into bankruptcy. They were rescued by a coalition of banks and suppliers that used to do business with them. Led by the Deutsche Bank, the group sacrificed its profits in order to bail out Daimler-Benz. Further investigation revealed that there were some Arab investors who wanted to buy out Daimler-Benz, but with the spirit of nationalism behind it, the bankers' coalition was quickly formed to prevent the Arab investors from taking over, which would have changed the German trademark to a non-German one. Furthermore, between the 1950s and 1970s in Europe, government after government nationalized failing industries of steel, coal and automobiles in the hope that state subsidies would help them regain international competitiveness. Even today, the agricultural subsidies provided by Europe and some other developed countries are hindering free and fair trade in our global village.

The nations from the developing countries were not fully involved in the two world wars, partly because they had no comparable ideology of their own. Even those who had, did not wish to impose it on others. Instead, both the victorious powers and the losing belligerents are now one "nation" by agreement, and impose the European-negotiated common ideology, and political and social culture, on the developing countries. Nowadays, all of the European countries have one voice, and when one of them has a problem with, say, Senegal or Mali or Nigeria or Libya, the full might of the European Union falls on that small country. This is worse than Stone Age barbarism. The answer for the developing countries should not lie in ideology per se; rather, it should involve the ability to choose whichever ideology suits their own environment. They could, while maintaining their social cohesion, add the European "spirit of nationalism" to produce a higher culture, whose diverse elements will successfully blend into a richer synthesis. Why not, as long as this will not lead to a dispirited society that is not sure of its own identity? If you are worried about your identity, then you have the spirit of nationalism in you. If you have no spirit of nationalism, then you must not aspire to lead others in your nation. The genie of nationalism, which started in Europe, is out of control and not easy to stop. The leaders of every nation must be nationalists or else the nation in question withers and dies. The leader who embezzles public money and takes it to another nation (which will use it for its own development) is not being patriotic to his nation, and should be punished with the same degree of punishment given to armed robbers in any country. The leaders should be accountable to the public for their actions and for the manner in which they carry out their responsibilities. They should also cooperate fully and honestly within a controlled system, such as a suitable level of overview and scrutiny appropriate to their particular office.

High-Trust Societies

It is generally believed that the greatest economic efficiency has been from the groups of individuals who, because they live in a pre-existing moral community, are able to work together efficiently. Such communities can share ethical values, and together can form organizations that will work for a common purpose. Because they adopt common norms as a whole, they can trust one another based on those shared sets of ethical norms. Trust, according to Davidow and Malone (1992), is the expectation that arises within a community of regular, honest and cooperative behaviour, based on commonly shared norms on the part of other members of that community.

Where a society is regarded as a high-trust society, social capital has inevitably emerged. Social capital is the ability of groups of individuals to work together without fear of one another. It can be found in families, social groups or in the largest of all groups, a nation. Doing business in such environments costs less and people are able to establish and properly manage modern, large-scale, international, competitive industries. Germany and Japan are group-oriented societies and are good examples of high-trust societies. Although America is often regarded as an individualistic society, people there have always belonged to voluntary organizations and community structures to which members are loyal. Such social capital has helped these three countries establish the largest industries in the world. These large industries have, in turn, brought back to their home countries the huge profits that make them the greatest capitalist nations on earth. Other countries that have social capital include South Korea, Holland, Sweden and the UK. In the absence of colonization, these countries with social capital are able to form gigantic corporations that bring back huge profits to their people.

Examples of these historically successful companies are:

USA	General Motors, Chevron
Germany	Mercedes Benz, VW Cars
Japan	Mitsubishi, Hitachi
South Korea	Hyundai Motor Company, Samsung Electric

	Company, Lucky Goldstar
Holland	Shell Petroleum
United Kingdom	Shell Petroleum

A high-trust society can organize its workforce on a group-oriented basis. With the trust embedded in the social structure, the senior ones look after the junior ones, and vice versa. Workers find their work very satisfying and give their full loyalty to the organization employing them; hence, corporations are professionally managed and, as such, these countries have been able to develop large, modern and professionally managed organizations. The only similarity among these countries can be traced to their highly developed sense of communal solidarity. This means that any of today's developing countries that can develop such cultural characteristics can become an industrialized nation tomorrow. Therefore, the problem with less developed countries is nothing to do with either their geographical locations or their people's skin colour. It is not even to do with past colonization experiences. After all, the Germans lost two devastating wars which destroyed their country, yet within two decades of the last world war they became the second largest economy in the world.

The world is like a marketplace, my grandmother told me. International competition is merely a civilized battlefield in a marketplace. Large-scale production leads to economies of scale and decreases in production costs. All things being equal, when two or more international companies are competing for markets in a certain country, the competing corporations take a crack at each other by lowering the prices of their goods. The others hit back by lowering their prices too. This goes on and on. At some point, their prices are below their production costs. The corporation or country that wins the contest is the one that produces at the lowest cost – namely the large-scale industries that enjoy economies of scale. Most of them are from the high-trust societies. They have this advantage and usually take control of the overseas markets they compete for. Obviously, there is nothing wrong with nations forming large-scale organizations in order to compete at the international level. It is only wrong when these gigantic corporations start meddling in the internal politics of their host developing countries, or start bribing their way to getting contracts, thereby encouraging bribery and corruption in the poor country.

Low-Trust Societies

Karl Marx's speculations never got beyond the daydreaming stage. In his imagined utopian state, he thought poverty would be eliminated and that health, wealth and happiness would be available for everyone. He forecast honest judges presiding in honest courts. He foresaw common ownership of the means of production and that people would enjoy comfort and luxury through their ownership of that means of production. These dreams would have been possible in a high-trust society, but the evil of capitalism did not allow this to crystallize. A socialist society can only be ushered in where there is a very high degree of trust. With the exception of a few countries, socialism has gone. Capitalism breeds low-trust people because everyone is struggling to maintain his or her dignity by using his or her fellow beings. Looking at it from another angle, capitalism breeds a low-trust world because, with the spirit of nationalism, every nation is struggling to maintain superiority over other nations.

Such low trust is a barrier to industrialization and rapid economic development. In low-trust societies, trust is usually found in families; hence the word familism. Familism cultures would find it difficult to establish large organizations that can compete internationally. They establish mainly small family businesses because the individuals cannot trust one another beyond their family circles. For them, parochialism came before nationalism. This does not mean, however, that states with such cultures cannot prosper anyway; they can. After all, some countries such as Taiwan, France, Italy and China are all familist states. But their biggest problem is raising capital for large-scale businesses. In Taiwan, for example, there is a cultural propensity to be one's own boss rather than work as a subordinate or member of a team. This is why Taiwan lacks large firms. Although about 20% of its firms employ more than 1,000 employees, 80% of all the firms in Taiwan employ fewer than 20 people. Taiwan, China, Italy and most African countries are familistic societies, and state intervention is often the only way such nations can build large-scale industries. Just like states building more schools and universities in order to rectify a deficit in human knowledge, when there is a deficit in social capital or a lack of employment opportunities, the state can make good the shortfall by pumping capital into the establishment of industries. After all, we all know about Taiwan's rapid economic rise in the 1980s. What we do not know is that in the 1980s, of the ten largest industries in Taiwan seven were public enterprises. So, beyond the provision of capital (because many businessmen and women want the type of businesses that give quick profits), the state has no choice but to step in and develop strategic industries.

Cultural Change

No culture is complete by itself. There is usually room for cultural change in any society. It was the integration of national cultures that resulted in the present world civilization. As Howard (2007) says:
It had, after all, been the cross-fertilization of national and cultural traditions that had created the astonishing richness of European civilization during the half millennium between the fifteenth and the twentieth centuries – the intermingling of Italian and French and Spanish and English and German to constitute a common European cultural core.

A culture can change from good to bad, or vice versa. According to Fukuyama (1995), Japan's confrontation with Western culture after the arrival of Commodore Perry's "black ships" in 1853 paved the way for the Meiji Restoration of Japan and its subsequent industrialization. London in the 1980s was different from the London of the 2000s. In the 80s, a lost wallet full of money and other valuables would be returned to the owner at his/her address, or the owner might receive a letter asking him/her to collect the wallet from someone or from the police or train station. It might go from public hands to the police; yet, you could be sure that the contents of the wallet would remain intact. But today, the wallet would not even reach the police station, far less come back to the owner. Another example of cultural change concerns the power and influence of media, particularly television, over its audience. Many developing countries are rapidly Westernizing, faster than ever before. Technological advancement in television has made it possible for people in developing countries to watch Western movies, news, football, etc. The resultant effect is cultural change. Unfortunately, many of the changes are not ones that could lead to social capital, trust or an emerging spirit of nationalism, and therefore, are not conducive to economic advancement. It is through the acceptance and domestication of other cultures that a country can become great and of any importance in the global village, but it must copy the good ones. America is great today because it is made up of people from different nations who brought their own cultures with them. For example, the Jewish scientists who fled from Nazi Germany to America made a formidable contribution to allied victory in the Second World War.

Small is Better

However, people who do not trust one another end up cooperating only under a system of formal rules and regulations. Obeying such rules and regulations helps them to become high-trust societies, and somehow to achieve social capital. In such a society there is still an alternative industrial policy. This alternative is what some writers now call "Industrial Districts". Applying the principles of industrial districts, a country or local authority area can still compete internationally and reap the same benefits that large-scale industries usually enjoy. After all, the basic idea behind the development of mass production is "economies of scale". It is usually considered necessary when an industry requires a large amount of capital for fixed assets such as machinery. As Kitching explains:

Up to a certain size of operation the volume of output from that fixed capital (we might think of an example such as the production of strip steel) grows proportionately with the size of the investment. But beyond a certain point, which varies with the technology being employed, the volume of output grows more than proportionately to the capital investment required to produce it – hence, the cost in terms of fixed capital of each unit of output falls. Since highly "capital-intensive" industrial technologies tend also to reduce the amount of labour employed per unit of output as the scale of production grows, then, all other things being equal, the enterprise using such techniques stands to reduce all costs per unit of output and thus to gain more profit per unit of output as output rises, and hence more profit overall (Kitching, 1989: 12).

But the likelihood of economies of scale occurring varies from one product to another, from one sector to another and from one place to another. The economies-of-scale concept has not worked for some countries that have industrialized their farming methods. In particular, if the economies of scale had worked in the farming sectors in Europe, no one would be talking about agricultural subsidies, and the governments in these countries would not have to support farmers financially. Labour-intensive farming cannot compete with the mechanized farming in Europe, not because of economies of scale, but rather because of the subsidies the latter receives from its respective government.
But let us look at what Kitching wrote about some non-agricultural consumer products:

If, for example, the industrial process involved is a very complex one in which it is technically difficult to design or utilize machinery to replace human labour, and if, in addition, there is for some reason an abundance of labour seeking employment and wages are low, then it may be more profitable for an enterprise to continue to operate in small units and to increase production by multiplying the units rather than by enlarging the scale of production in big plants. This has been the case in the production of electronic and optical equipment in Japan and other parts of Southeast Asia (Kitching, 1989).

This system of production (with certain principles) is called the "industrial district model". Italy is well known for applying the principle of industrial districts, and the industrial districts model has enabled it to achieve industrialized status in Europe.

Industrial Districts

Industrial districts are much more than a concentration of industries within the same sector, operating within a limited geographical area. According to Frank Pyke and Werner Sengenberger, industrial districts are not just collections of disparate firms and services organized together on what the British call Industrial Estates and the French call Zones Industrielles. What is specific and different is the way that the firms are organized together according to certain principles. These principles are discussed below. Meanwhile, the industrial districts model is an initiative aimed at learning from the Italian industrial districts experience. It encourages the concentration of small- and medium-sized businesses in a particular geographical location so that they can enjoy economies of scale. Small industries become the backbone of the local economy, but they are developed on the basis of certain principles, ethics and norms. By obeying these rules and norms, the culture of businesses and the community is shaped. One of the key rules is cooperation among the businesses, workers and unions, which results in what some writers call "collective efficiency". This means that the society's norms, expectations and ethics change from the Italians' former low-trust society orientation to a high-trust society. The lesson here is that values, and formal legal and customary rules, can shape people's behaviours within society. The Italian principles of the industrial districts method of production yielded not only economic success through advantageous access to low-cost factors of production, but also brought social capital into the communities. In addition, some research carried out during the 1970s on industrial districts revealed that a productive structure, under certain conditions, is capable of producing goods for the international markets at competitive prices. Brusco and Sabel (1981) went on to say that ten lathe machines in ten different rooms can be operated as efficiently as ten lathe machines that are put together in one room.

A typical Italian industrial district model was in Modena. Modena is one of the provinces of Emilia-Romagna, in which the features of the industrial districts model appeared very clearly. The experience of Modena presents a challenge to the school of thought that maintains that industrialization can only be achieved by channeling all efforts towards large-scale modern industries. This model of development is now well known to development scholars as a case where industrialization has been characterized by the presence of many small businesses. Many small firms in the Modena area were made to concentrate on the joint form of a "productive system". Not being a mere concentration of small businesses, they had certain attributes that helped them to achieve economies of scale. These principles are:

- Geographical proximity of the businesses;
- Sectoral specialization;
- Predominance of small- and medium-sized firms;
- Close inter-firm collaboration that leads to collective efficiency;
- Inter-firm competition based on innovation rather than lowering wages;
- A shared social and cultural identity which facilitates trust between firms, employers and skilled workers;
- Full involvement and assistance from the local government.

Industrial success is not credited to one individual firm. Its strength lies in clustering, which opens up flexibility and efficiency that individual producers can rarely attain. Industrial districts did not only emerge in the Third Italy; they are also found in other parts of the globe including Baden-Wurttemberg in Germany, West Jutland in Denmark, South West Flanders in Belgium, the Sino Valley in Brazil, Ludhiana and Tiruppur in India, and Toyota City in Japan, among others. A number of local authorities world-wide have been pursuing this line of industrialization and some call it "regeneration". It is high time other developing countries started exploring the industrial districts model.

Geographical proximity

Industrial districts' principles require the clustering of many small businesses close together. It may lead to endogenous regional development and a territorial division of labour. Before its conception, however, the first question that often comes to mind is, how can the people of a locality make the most of local resources and special features in their area in order to set in motion a particular local development process? In fact, before the advent of industrial districts, some regional and local governments have often tried to attract new firms and new jobs by out-competing one another, by promising international companies low costs of production and the provision of a favourable business climate. But attracting firms by offering them the carrot of financial incentives has often failed to generate a lasting solution, because firms tend to leave after enjoying the period of favourable conditions.

The physical proximity of small firms not only benefits the community but also acts as the seedbed for an exchange of ideas across the businesses concerned. As such, the industrial district attempts to commit enterprises to continuous local and regional development, as well as to making the development of supportive institutions more effective.

Sectoral Specialization

In industrial districts, firms operate mainly in traditional sectors. In those sectors, however, the developing countries are expected to have a comparative advantage too. Firms cluster within the region and the region becomes known for specific sectors and activities. The most common sectors represented in the Third Italy are textiles, shoes, tiles, furniture and mechanical engineering. In West Jutland in Denmark, the specialization is in garments and furniture. Baden Wurttemberg of Germany specializes in metalworking and mechanical engineering, while South West Flanders' sectoral specialization includes textiles, wood and furniture. Let us look at sectoral specialization in Brazil. Brazil's Sino Valley specializes in shoemaking. According to Schmidt (1993), the area was described as a "super cluster" because the region stood out for its variety of firms that were involved in the backward and forward activities of shoe manufacturing. Over 500 local firms attracted the attention of exporters. The number of firms increased because of the various stages and inputs required in the production of shoes, such as uppers, heels, soles, insoles, eyelets, dyes and glues. Other firms in the area included export agents, designers, producers and service units. They all followed the principles of industrial districts, which helped them to reap the benefits usually enjoyed only by the large multinational corporations. Similarly, in a locality with fruit and vegetable potential, food industries in such districts will be producing things like tomatoes, pineapples, oranges, lemons, and grapefruit juices, tomato purée and mango pulp. To do this will involve a number of ancillary industries and will create employment opportunities in the locality.

Role of Regional or Local Governments

Regional and local governments have vital roles to play in the development of local economies. The council is an agency that can pilot the district towards ideal dynamic, social and economic systems. The first question that comes to mind is: what efforts are being made in order to stimulate the concentration of small companies in the locality? The answer is that the government has to create an enabling environment by making the right policy that helps entrepreneurs set up and develop their businesses in the locality – an initiative aimed at learning from the Italian industrial districts' experience by encouraging the development of small and medium enterprises in its locality.

The first step in creating an enabling environment is for the government to ensure the existence of a proper infrastructure and services such as water supply, communication facilities, good roads and constant electricity supply. The second step is to establish industrial estates and provide soft credits and training facilities for the small businesses.

Provision of Soft Credit

Investigations reveal that the local bank in the Third Italy is an organism born and bred in the district, and is very closely linked with local entrepreneurs (and often with other local social and political lobbies) and deeply involved in local life, which it knows in detail and to which it gives direction to a considerable extent.

The local banks in the Third Italy paid more attention to the personal qualities of the applicants than the viability of their investment projects. They were not asking for collateral. Instead, the bank managers knew the individuals personally and could assess their ability to pay back any money borrowed. They could easily assess their clients' capability of achieving their goals. The interest rates charged in the Third Italy by local banks to district firms were no different from that elsewhere. In developing countries, however, one would suggest that there must be a remarkable difference in rates of interest between the local banks and the commercial banks. To be able to charge lower interest rates, the local or community bank should look for funds overseas where the interest rates are very low. Sometimes, there are overseas donors that may not charge any interest. However, the local government has a role to play in helping them to secure sources of funding. It can also help them to create loan guarantee schemes/cover. This guarantee cover will enable the firms to borrow money with ease from the banks. Loan consortia are usually developed by unions who give their members loans from time to time, and the local government should encourage the formation of such unions. Another pro-active measure is investing in human resources. Training prospective workers to acquire one skill or another will be useful for the small businesses in the area, and some residents may even decide to set up their own small business.

Provision of Real Services

Local government assistance is what some writers call "real services". Real services are supportive services that involve supplying firms (in return for a small payment) with the services and goods they require instead of giving them money to buy them on the open market. The charges they pay are relatively small when compared with the market. They include things like the provision of information regarding the technical standards enforced by law in various foreign countries for those districts wishing to export their products and services. Other information provided can be on machinery, potential markets, sources of soft loans and innovation. A real service might also be the testing of manufacturers' inputs and outputs. Government laboratories would be able to test the entrepreneurs' products to ensure they met international and national standards. Another real service is the translation of tender documents. Information about tenders in foreign countries can be obtained from the Ministry of Foreign Trade or the Chamber of Commerce. The local government has to make provisions that will enable these documents to be translated for the local business community.

Corruption, Transparency and Governance

Corruption involves the act of bribery among other practices. Bribery is a gift of money used to persuade someone to do something improper, morally wrong or illegal. It can be the use of public office for private gain. Corruption exists everywhere in the world, in the private as well as the public sector. It exists in the developed countries as well as in the developing countries, but is at a lower level in the former. It hinders the social and economic development of any nation where it is practiced. On the other hand, corruption is an outcome of weak governance, because it is more likely to occur where state or local government capability, accountability and control systems are weak. Incidence of corruption varies from one culture to another. It is so vast an area that it is only possible to mention a few issues here:

Government Contracts: Bribes can influence the choice of contractors that would supply public goods and services to the government. Vastly inflated contracts are awarded to the relatives or cronies of officials in return for large kickbacks. Corruption could cause the lowering of the quality of infrastructure facilities, for example, where a contractor pays a lot in bribes before he/she gets the contract, he/she is likely to pay another kickback to the inspector whether or not the work is of a good standard. In that case, he/she may choose to hand over substandard work and "settle" with the inspector instead.

International Corporations: It is now an open secret that most corruption in developing countries has links with the big corporations from the industrialized countries. The First World is the source of many Third World bribes. It is a well-known fact that, for example, multinational oil corporations pay government officials bribes in order to win oil contracts in developing countries.

Distortions of Government Expenditure: Corrupt governments spend less on health and education and more on large, unnecessary expenditures such as fighter aircraft, where the government officials' interests will be protected and the bribes obtainable are large. Fighter aircraft may not be as important as health and education, but because the ministers or other officials are getting kickbacks, the project must go ahead.

Public Revenues: Bribes can be used to avoid or reduce the amount of taxes or fees due for collection by government officials from private parties. Such reductions in government revenue also affect the government's planned services to the public.

Influencing Outcomes of Legal and Regulatory Processes: Bribes can alter outcomes of the legal process by unduly favouring one party over another in court cases or other legal matters.

Embezzlement: Siphoning public money into private accounts is more harmful to the common man than the actions of a poor thief who, as a result of unemployment (where the state does not give any benefits), steals another person's possessions. The poor thief is stoned, imprisoned or killed, but the government thieves get away with their crimes. For instance, according to Western newspapers, within 30 years Nigerian leaders looted over £155 billion of oil revenue, and as at 2005 about £55 billion of private Nigerian assets was languishing in overseas bank accounts. A UK newspaper, the Daily Telegraph of 25 June 2005, claimed that the amount stolen or misused by corrupt Nigerian rulers amounted to £220 billion as at that date. Imagine if a large fraction of this amount had been used to establish industries, creating millions of job opportunities, the graduate unemployment rate would not have been so high, and many Nigerians would not have left their country in search of jobs abroad.

Impeding Foreign Investment: Foreign investors are put off in an environment or society that sees corruption as an acceptable norm. Corruption-ridden countries are lousy competitors in the global economy because bribes and kickbacks make the costs of doing business too high. For example, a case where investors are asked to pay bribes before their applications are treated or even before they are allowed to commence business, can put off potential investors.

Corruption Stalls the Careers of Politicians

Corruption scandals have uprooted some of the world's leaders in democratic countries. In France, investigations of numerous kickbacks have ousted ministers and several mayors, with the left (the Socialist Party) tainted by a reputation for corruption. For decades, Italian voters tolerated the corruption of the Christian Democrats and later, their Socialist allies. But around the collapse of the Soviet Union, the Italians realized that their taxes were being increased in order to pay for the extensive public works that were exorbitantly costly due to bribes and kickbacks, and that, in fact, most of the projects did not even work at all. A newly formed political party, then called the Forza Italia Party, won the 1994 elections on a clean-up pledge. Before its victory, however, a team of magistrates had begun to investigate more than 3,000 politicians and businessmen. The investigation devastated what was once the ruling class of Italy, which had ruled the country for about 40 years. More than 1,000 of them were jailed. In Brazil, President Fernando Collor de Mello was impeached and removed from office (even though he was acquitted two years later) on corruption charges, and his campaign fundraiser, Paulo Cesar Farias, was jailed. In South Korea, two former military rulers – Presidents Chun Doo Hwan and Roh Tae Woo – were jailed for bribery and the instigation of the Kwangju massacre.

But in Bolivia, punishment for corruption is not just imprisonment. Anyone elected to local and municipal office must sign an anti-corruption pledge and agree to show up in the village square if he or she violates it. In the village square, every member of the affected community will take a turn flogging the bare buttocks of crooked officials with a nettle branch. Afterwards, the offenders will be driven out of the town. In Taiwan, soon after his father's death, Chiang Ching-Kuo took over power in the 1970s and had 45 government officials arrested for customs violations, including members of the feared Military Intelligence branch. Another 20 officials, plus his own personal secretary, were jailed for bribery (Eigler, 1988). The purpose was to establish an image of incorruptibility in his government (Wade, 1990).

A crackdown on corruption is a badge of modernity and a sign that a society is advancing towards joining the more civilized world. A combination of an inquisitive press and an independent and morally minded judiciary can also make such crackdowns possible.

Merit

After getting rid of the corrupt officials, Ching-Kuo (Taiwan) was faced with the problem of appointing the right people to his cabinet. Unlike his father, who wanted to bring native Taiwanese into senior positions within the state, Ching-Kuo foresaw the danger of taking mainly his Taiwanese kinsmen or tribe into his cabinet without minding their suitability for the positions. In his appointments, he placed emphasis on "cleanness" of reputations and instilled a fear in the members of his cabinet of taking bribes. He also barred them from appearing in places like bars, expensive restaurants and dancehalls. The lesson here was that tribalism or nepotism had no place in him choosing his team. Even when Ching-Kuo died in January 1988, President Lee succeeded him and strictly followed the "cleanness" of reputations in the promotion of native Taiwanese. One can now see why Taiwan made rapid economic progress during this period.

Patriotism

Although there was still a 10% level of kickbacks in public work projects, bribery was limited to imported items that were not essential for the economic development of Taiwan. Customs took bribes on foodstuffs but not on industrial goods, as they were important for economic development. Even the 10% on public works projects would only take place through overcharging for correctly built structures. This means that Taiwan's type of bribe is less damaging to its economic development.

Institutional Inefficiency

Corruption is most prevalent in a society that has some forms of institutional inefficiency such as local government and municipal authority without effective governance systems, and weak legislative and judicial systems. Without putting proper control systems in place (checks and balances), the officials and elected members are indirectly encouraged to be corrupt. In each tier of government, a Standards Committee should be set up and trained. The Committee would be responsible for advising on the adoption of a code setting out the Standards of Conduct expected from elected members and all government officials. A Scrutiny and Overview team should also be set up. Scrutiny and overview is more than a mere performance review. It is proactive rather than reactive, and is prospective and retrospective, creative and constructive, as well as critical and blame-seeking. Contract Procedural Rules have to be set out in the Constitution. Where these measures are already in place, the political will has to be found in order to ensure their implementation. Corrupt and inefficient institutions are intrinsically linked, in the sense that they feed upon each other. Therefore, curbing institutional inefficiency will help a country overcome corruption, and vice versa.

Revenue Reform Programme

A sound revenue reform programme allows the government to close all loopholes for corruption. For example, in Mozambique, the UK Department for International Development (DFID) provided long-term support, about £30 million, with which the country embarked on three major revenue reform programmes: the modernization of customs operations; support to develop IT systems; and preparatory work to establish a Central Revenue Authority. As a result of these improvements, by 2005 goods started clearing at the ports forty times faster, and there is now a more effective anti-smuggling control system in place, which has led to increased revenues for the government. There should be proper public financial management systems in place that will ensure good revenue and expenditure reports.

International Resolution on Multinational Activities

In a speech at the World Bank in April 2007, the Head of Nigeria's Economic and Financial Crime Commission, Nuhu Ribadu, said that he had seen the multinationals and big oil companies play by the rules elsewhere but behave badly in Nigeria and Africa generally. Also, in the UK's Financial Times of Monday 1 June 2009, Michael Peel wrote that Jeffrey Tesler, who worked for an international building consortium, had been accused of giving bribes to Nigerian officials up to the sum of $130 million to win a contract of a $6 billion gas plant in southern Nigeria. This, according to Mr Peel, happened between 1995 and 2004. Back home in Britain, a 2002 British anti-graft law made it an offence to bribe foreign public officials. But regulations made by the multinationals' home countries are not enough to deter them. This is because judgements in their own countries will always go in their favour. Developing countries need similar actions to be taken to the one described in Chapter One – when the slave trade was abolished by the British government, its Royal Navy helped to police the trade in the high sea by stopping other nations' ships from engaging in it. Obviously, such multinational activities bring cultural changes in many developing countries, Nigeria being one example. When the people at the top receive bribes from multinational corporations, they have no moral authority to tell other people in the country not to accept bribes too.

Regulations that make it mandatory for all multinationals doing business in developing countries to disclose all payments made to governments and government officials can limit graft. The United Nations can pass such a resolution and ensure that proper monitoring and enforcement systems are in place. This will help to close all loopholes that permit illicit gains through bribery. Maybe the role of the International Court of Justice can be expanded to include such criminal activities. The new legal regime that is emerging has created the International Criminal Court, but the spectrum of this international legal regime should cover not only terrorism and human rights but, essentially, corruption and money-laundering from the developing countries to the developed countries.

Anti-Corruption Reforms

In the 1990s Hong Kong and Singapore established anti-corruption commissions that proved very successful in educating their communities, as well as in investigating and preventing corruption. Georgia is another good example of the importance of building good governance systems. According to statistics, this is the country that has achieved the most marked reduction in corruption in recent years. The UK DFID also helped Georgia to implement a range of measures, such as reforms to strengthen public finance management, the establishment of a Supreme Audit Institution, and the dismissal of large numbers of corrupt police, and tax and customs officials. Sierra Leone is another country where the UK DFID assisted in fighting corruption. The help provided included technical support that created overseas bodies such as the Anti-Corruption and Parliament Units, improved financial management systems, and worked with civil society to provide information to citizens so that they could hold the government to account. It introduced Public Expenditure Tracking Surveys (PETS) in 2002, which have helped to reduce the "leakages" in the delivery of essential drugs to hospitals, for example. Finally, on 4 May 2007 the former Zambian President was ordered by the High Court in London to return $46 million in assets stolen from Zambia. The DFID assisted the government of Zambia to ensure that no one was immune to investigation and prosecution for corrupt activities. This was a wonderful move by the British government, but it was not enough. Efforts to extend such assistance to the people, rather than the corrupt government, of other African countries could go a long way to stop corruption in Africa, and in particular, other civilized developed countries of our global village should follow the pace set by the British.

Existence of a Free Press

The existence of investigative reporting is very important. Some countries have libel laws that protect politicians and public officials. These must be opposed and stopped. It is important to provide information, raising awareness to improve transparency and safeguard citizens' freedom of expression. Disseminating information about corruption is a powerful way of letting people know what is going on in their country. By 2006, nearly 70 countries around the globe had adopted comprehensive Freedom of Information Acts to facilitate access to records held by their government bodies, and another 50 countries were in the process of doing so (Banisar, 2006). The question is, therefore, why does such looting exist in the first place?

Code of Conduct

It is essential that there is a general code of conduct to be obeyed by all elected government members. General principles of a code of conduct might be as follows:

Selflessness
Members should serve only the public interest and should never improperly confer an advantage or disadvantage on any person.

Honesty and Integrity
Members should not place themselves in situations where their honesty and integrity may be questioned. They should not behave improperly and should, on all occasions, avoid the appearance of such behaviour.

Objectivity
Members should make decisions on merit, including when making appointments, awarding contracts, or recommending individuals for rewards or benefits.

Accountability
Members should be accountable to the public for their actions and the manner in which they carry out their responsibilities. They should cooperate fully and honestly with any scrutiny appropriate to their particular office.

Openness
Members should be as open as possible about their actions and those of their authorities, and should be prepared to give reasons for those actions.

Personal Judgment
Members should take account of the views of others, including their political groups, but should ultimately reach their own conclusions on the issues before them and act in accordance with those conclusions.

Respect for Others
Members should promote equality by not discriminating unlawfully against any person, and by treating people with respect, regardless of their tribe,

age, religion, gender or disabilities. They should respect the impartiality and integrity of all statutory officers and other employees.

Duty to Uphold the Law
Members should uphold laws and, on all occasions, act in accordance with the trust that the public is entitled to place in them.

Stewardship
Members should do whatever they are able to ensure that their authorities use their resources prudently and in accordance with the law.

Leadership
Members should promote and support these principles by leadership and by example, and should act in a way that secures or preserves public confidence.

Improper Influence on Staff
Members should avoid improper influence on staff with delegated authority to make decisions. Such influence might lead the officers to make unlawful decisions.

Members are required to give a written undertaking, that in performing their functions they will observe the Code of Conduct. The above list merely sets out the principles, as a code usually contains more detailed mandatory requirements.

It is a well-known fact that most reported corruption in developing countries takes place at the local government level, especially in a nation that does not have major projects being undertaken at a national level. For this reason, it will be appropriate to discuss in this book a model local government system that can guarantee good governance to the people. That system is the British model.

The British Local Government System

Confidence in local democracy is a cornerstone of the British way of life. Such confidence in local democracy can only be achieved in many developing countries when the elected members of the local governments are seen to be living up to the high standards which the public expect of them.

Historical Perspective

In order to understand the present local government system in Britain, it is necessary to appreciate how the system has evolved over the centuries. In the seventeenth century, that is, some 200 years before the emergence of political parties, there were the magistrates or Justices of the Peace (JPs), who were appointed as local agents in each town to represent the king. The JPs governed themselves through corporations established by a royal charter and had the right to determine their own system of government.

The responsibility for overseeing or initiating necessary local improvements was in the hands of these local Justices of the Peace. The local improvements included maintenance of all the roads not maintained by trusts. They were also responsible for the upkeep of law and order in their areas. But the officials were often lazy and incompetent. Many of them were corrupt and only interested in lining their own pockets rather than looking after the interests of the townspeople.

On the other hand, some towns had reform-minded leaders, and in 1831 they realized that it was clear that a new and more democratic system of town government was needed to replace the corrupt municipal corporations. First, they took action through Special Acts of Parliament called Local Improvement Acts, which enabled them to take steps to improve their towns. Then, in 1835 came the Municipal Corporations Act, which reorganized the existing 178 boroughs into 78 multi-purpose elected local authorities. They were not concerned with the administration of justice, and from then on a common democratic system emerged, which became the foundation of our present-day local government. The ratepayers, who were the property owners in each town, elected a town council. The councillors elected were responsible for those services authorized by the Local Improvement Acts, such as water supply, policing the town and street lighting. The new councils held meetings in public and submitted their accounts each year to an audit. The audit checked that the rates collected had been properly spent. The councillors elected the council leader or mayor and appointed the town clerk and treasurers. Having summarized the past, it is now easy for me to demonstrate how the present UK local governments operate.

Present System

Determined to enhance the performance of councils in the UK, some general objectives have emerged, as follows:

- Better services;
- Quicker decisions;
- Clearer and more accountable leadership;
- A more transparent and open system of decision-making;
- Increased community involvement;
- Greater opportunities for ward councillors to represent their constituents;
- Better partnership working;
- More democratic debate within the regular council meetings on matters of real importance and interest to the local community.

The British government believed that all this could be achieved through strong leadership, a challenging scrutiny structure and ward councillors who have a real and meaningful role within their communities. Consequently, the 1998 White Paper Modern Local Government: In Touch with the People was produced. It proposed three possible management structures for local authorities. These models were subsequently included in the Local Government Act 2000. The Act gave the councils three model choices in terms of reorganizing their decision-making process, as follows:

1. Cabinet and Leader
2. Elected Mayor with a Cabinet
3. Elected Mayor with Council Manager

As a result, many local governments carried out a public consultation exercise in 2001. After taking into account the views expressed by the electorates, they chose to adopt the Cabinet and Leader model. Again, this model was the option chosen by most local governments across the country. Since then, they have all drafted new constitutions based on this model.

The Council

The council is the sovereign body to which all other parts of our model are accountable. It is where all councillors meet together to debate and agree on matters of major policy. Councillors have the opportunity to question cabinet members and scrutinize chairmen on topical issues, and the opposition can include items of their choice on the agenda. They usually have four meetings each year. This is known as opposition business. All council meetings are open to the public and members of the public are encouraged to attend.

The Council Leader

The leader of the council, in other words the chairman, is a councillor. He or she has been elected to the position of leader by the councillors. The leader is the coordinator who chairs the executive meetings. The leader may, at any time, convene special meetings on particular issues. The term of reference and membership of such meetings can be specified by the leader when convening such meetings. The leader may also recommend as follows:

- The settlement of conflicts between services;
- Action to achieve declared policies and guidelines;
- Advice and guidance to be given to the council, its committees, sub-committees or panels upon any matter within the purview of the council, which will assist those bodies to discharge the council's functions in accordance with their terms of reference.

Leader's Job Description

Using one of London's local governments as an example, the leader's job description is as follows:

1. To provide leadership in the development and maintenance of an active and participatory local democracy.
2. To chair the executive. To ensure that the council's decision -making process functions effectively and that decisions made by

the executive take into account all relevant factors and reflect the council's commitment to open government and equal opportunity.

3. To ensure delivery of the council's overall vision.

4. To implement, working with the Chief Executive, strategies and policies approved by the council and reflecting the views of the public as set out in the Community Plan (delegating work to other executive members where necessary).

5. To exercise a monitoring role regarding performance and budgets, to ensure progress towards meeting the executive's key objectives.

6. To maintain a clear communications strategy.

7. To ensure that executive members and directorates work together effectively.

8. To ensure that non-executive members are informed on and engaged in the council's work.

9. To act as the key spokesperson of the council on major strategic and policy issues. To work to maintain the council's positive image with members of the public and in the media and to show community leadership.

10. To represent the council on a range of external matters.

11. To act, at all times, with the highest standards of probity as defined by the Seven Principles of Public Life (as stated above), the Code of Conduct for Members and the Council's Protocol for Member-Officer Relations.

12. To always use the best interests of the people of the borough as a guide to actions.

The Cabinet

The cabinet is part of the executive. The cabinet members are appointed by the leader of the council. They are normally from the party that won the local government election. The cabinet deals with a lot of the business details of the provision of the council's services:

- Provides political direction and guidance to the council officers;
- Develops and consults on policy proposals;
- Proposes the council's budget;
- Delivers the council's priorities and services;
- Improves the council's performance;
- Creates and sustains effective partnerships;
- Responds to issues raised by the overview, and the scrutiny

committee and scrutiny panels;
- Links together the work of the council's new area of forums and community housing partnerships.

A cabinet can set up sub-committees to deal with specific issues such as Best Value. All cabinet members are accessible to other councillors and their individual and collective decisions may be open to scrutiny. The cabinet usually meets every three weeks. Their agendas for meetings are usually made available to the public at least five working days before each meeting. Their decisions are made available to the public within 48 hours of each meeting and minutes within ten working days. Also, members of the public can ask to present a deputation to the cabinet.

Call-In

The majority of decisions taken by the cabinet or by cabinet members are not implemented immediately. They are subject to the council's call-in process, which basically means that the decision can be reviewed before it is adopted. This works as follows:
- Decisions taken are published within 48 hours.
- Unless reasons for urgency can be demonstrated, councillors then have five working days to ask that a particular decision be reviewed (or called-in). Councillors have to give reasons for the call-in and provide an alternative course of action. Only the following can call items in:
  a) A minimum of seven councillors signing a call-in form;
  b) A scrutiny panel;
  c) The chairman of the scrutiny panel, providing the subject matter is within his/her panel's remit and (because of the call-in deadlines) it would not be possible to wait until the next meeting of that panel.

When a valid "call-in" is received, a meeting of the council's overview and scrutiny committee is arranged within 14 days of the end of that call-in period. That committee will consider the call-in request and then decide on one of three options:
1) Confirm the original decision (in which case the decision can be implemented immediately).
2) Refer the decision back to the decision-maker for reconsideration – they can either confirm the original decision or change it, and this can then be implemented.

3) Refer the matter to full council for consideration (it is expected that this will only be in the most exceptional circumstances). Council can either refer the matter back to the decision-maker with an alternative recommendation or confirm the original decision. If confirmed, the decision is implemented.

Deputation

The public may present the cabinet with deputations. These must be sponsored by a named councillor. Some councils require notice of at least five working days before the meeting. It must relate to a local government matter concerning the council. Where possible, the cabinet will respond immediately to the deputations at the meeting, but if this is not possible, the cabinet may refer the subject matter to the relevant director, cabinet member, scrutiny panel or committee for further consideration. The cabinet may also decide not to receive or refer the deputation to an appropriate committee, sub-committee or other body.

Petitions

Any person can send a petition to the cabinet, but must give the required notice before their next meeting. It must relate to a council matter in the local government area. A petition can be presented by not more than two persons, who do not address the cabinet but reply to questions from the cabinet.

Scrutiny

Scrutiny is a mechanism by which public accountability is exercised. Local governments make decisions on behalf of the people in their area and spend money intended for those people. Scrutiny therefore means holding the leader of the council and the executive councillors to account for decisions they take on behalf of the local people.

The Local Government Act 2000 brought in those arrangements that clearly defined a scrutiny role for elected members in holding council executives to account, and in scrutinizing the work of other agencies providing local services. All members of scrutiny committees are non-executive council members. There is a clear role distinction here – between the executive's roles in proposing and implementing policies, and the role of non-executive members in reviewing policy and scrutinizing executive decisions. In England and Wales, local government overview and scrutiny committees have the power to summon members of the executive and officers of the local government to answer questions, and are able to invite other persons to attend the meetings to give their views or submit evidence.

Let us look at how another London local government set up its scrutiny section. One of the lessons learned from the cabinet and leader arrangements was the need for scrutiny to have a stronger voice within the council and for the work of the panels to be better planned and coordinated. The local government introduced an overview and scrutiny committee comprising the chairmen of their six scrutiny panels. They also agreed that scrutiny had a responsibility to challenge and question the decisions of the cabinet and officers, whilst also playing a more proactive role in developing policy and improvements in the council's services. The council delegates much of its work to these policy committees, each of which concentrate on a particular area of the council's work and are responsible for determining the council's policy in these areas. Each panel has a chairperson who chairs its meetings, speaks and acts on its behalf, and liaises with relevant officers. They do not take decisions personally. The six scrutiny panels of our model local government are:

- Education, Skills and Learning
- Environment, Parks and Amenities
- Health
- Housing
- Social Services
- Special Projects

After consultation with the cabinet and corporate management board, the panels produce work programmes each year. Some of the programmes will give consideration to the cabinet's own proposal for the budget. The scrutiny panels and committees are not decision-making bodies but have an important role in working with the public to look at the effectiveness, responsiveness and efficiency of the council's services.

All panels are cross-party and opposition members chair two out of the six. The panels are encouraged to be non-partisan and creative in the way they approach their work. They can (and do) co-opt individuals, appoint independent experts, call witnesses and hold enquiries (some jointly involving two or more panels). The Education, Skills and Learning scrutiny panel, for example, has co-opted members from a number of religious faiths with schools in the local area (Roman Catholic, Church of England and the Jewish faith), plus they have elected representatives from parent governors. They are also entitled to attend meetings of the overview and scrutiny committee. The primary, secondary and college principals are also represented on this panel.

The Forward Plan

The Local Government Act 2000 requires each council to publish a Forward Plan every month. This plan contains the key decisions that the executive will be considering during the forthcoming four-month period. It is designed to give the public and councillors advance notice of the important decisions being taken by the council. It also provides an opportunity for people to have an input in the decision-making process. Key decisions in this local government are defined as a proposal which:

a) involves expenditure or savings of £250,000 or more; or
b) has a significant impact on the local community in one or more ways.

The plan is a public document and is available for inspection from libraries. It is published 14 days before it comes into operation. It sets out the decision to be taken, who will be consulted, the methods and timing of that consultation, and who will be taking that decision, plus the relevant documents relating to those issues.

Standards Committee

The Local Government Act 2000 requires every local authority to have a standards committee to monitor and promote good conduct on the part of councillors. The committee is the independent guardian of the public's interests in relation to councillor conduct.

The committee of this local government is made up of two independent members and four councillors, two from each major political party that is represented in the council. Its roles are to ensure high standards of conduct amongst members, provide training and to monitor compliance with the councillors' code of conduct. It is also intended that the standards committee will be able to investigate and determine allegations of member misconduct. It meets in public wherever possible and makes recommendations to full council.

There is also the Standards Board for England, which is responsible for promoting high ethical standards and investigating allegations that members' behaviour may have fallen short of the required standards. Any member of the public, a councillor, council officer or the standards committee may refer issues to the board.

Audit Committee

The council has an audit committee to promote and ensure the best practice for corporate governance, finance and probity. It is also responsible for preventing fraud and corruption, and arranging for the proper management of public funds.

Finally, to ensure that local government revenues are properly utilized, using the British system would enable developing countries to establish finance procedural rules, set up an overview and scrutiny committee, elect standards committee members and carry out a regular review of the constitution. This would guarantee accountability, transparency and good governance, hence the benefit of grass roots democracy.

CHAPTER THREE
Choosing an Industrialization Pathway

Appropriate Technology

In choosing an industrialization pathway, a country, local government or regional authority has to decide whether to promote the cottage industry, the small-medium industry (SMI), the large automated industry or a combination of all three. One important factor that may influence its choice is whether to go for import-substitution industrialization or export-led industrialization. Firstly, a decision has to be made as to whether to encourage labour-intensive or capital-intensive production. Where there is a need to combine capital- and labour-intensive technologies, the proportion of each is important. Above all, if the technologies are difficult, specialized skills may be required. An ability to master these skills is needed and may call for complex organization, market structuring, cultural orientation, etc. All these play an important role in choosing an appropriate technology pathway. Countries with a small population but with very high per capita income, such as Singapore, Kuwait or South Korea, where the national incomes far exceed the countries' current and future requirements, may choose the capital-intensive (automated) production pathway. But they must produce for export markets to succeed. On the other hand, developing countries such as Nigeria and Indonesia, with a large surplus of labour and very low per capita incomes, may think about a combination of the two: labour-intensive (small-to-medium scale) and capital-intensive industries. In fact, many developing countries attempting to achieve economic advancement make the wrong choices in selecting suitable technologies. Those not affected by this problem concentrate on labour-intensive light industries, thus exploiting their cheap labour.

A government is expected to be concerned with the social and economic needs of its people, such as employment, skills acquisition and environment, while the country's enterprises may only be interested in competitiveness, profit, growth or entry into specific markets. There is no single set of industrial strategies or appropriate technologies applicable for all local governments, state governments, regional governments or the whole country. This is primarily because factors such as population size, natural resource endowments, development levels and per capita incomes are so diverse. Each government will have to adopt its own strategy based on its identified priorities, and will have to decide for itself what it can achieve in the short term as well as the long term. In addition, other factors to take into consideration include available factor inputs, potential for mobilizing external technology, infrastructure development priorities, information and technical support, availability of financial resources to supplement these efforts and, above all, the spirit of nationalism. Due to this diverse array of considerations, governments may look at the following options in light of their chosen paths.

Import-Substitution Industrialization

The country produces articles domestically instead of importing them. It is generally accepted among leading industrial development specialists that import substitution in the early stages of any country's industrialization programme is a necessary first step. Without this, the success of Southeast Asia might not have been possible. Import substitution has also helped to foster the rapid expansion in manufacturing seen in countries such as Mexico, Brazil, Turkey and the Philippines.

It is at the first step of industrialization that protective measures can be justified, including tariffs to protect infant industries. It is during this period that essential skills are acquired, infrastructure developed and the technological basis underpinned. Such protective measures will lead to higher potential for the acquisition of more sophisticated technology and prospects for an expanding virtuous circle of international markets, incomes and reinvestment. This encourages people to learn by doing. It protects infant industries against foreign competition; it creates employment opportunities; and it helps to redistribute income in the society. It is more beneficial if the country has a large internal market. Arguably, it reduces continuous outflow of foreign exchange. This last benefit is not certain because unless project screening and evaluation can ensure that commercial and economic profitability criteria are met, the net savings of foreign exchange over the lifetime of any project may be negative. However, the benefits enumerated above can only be achieved if the government uses protective measures, for example, in the form of import duties, outright bans on imports of some items, quotas and industrial licensing to protect infant industries.

Protective measures have been used since 1599 by the Europeans and Americans to enable themselves to develop. Four hundred and ten years on, there are still protective measures being taken by the developed countries. These range from trade controls to farm subsidies. Currently, the wealthy nations spend about $370 billion a year on all forms of farm support. Agricultural trade with a heavy subsidy component is not free trade. How can poor farmers in developing countries compete when farmers in rich countries can sell their goods at prices below the cost of production?

In particular, four West African countries, Benin, Burkina Faso, Mali and Togo – about ten million people in all – depend on cotton for a large proportion of their national income. These farmers grow the world's best cotton, yet their low prices are not competitive with cotton prices in the US. This is because the American government has been subsidizing the 30,000 American cotton farmers, and the poor cotton farmers in Africa cannot compete. Writing in the UK's newspaper The Independent on 2 August 2004, shortly after the WTO agreement, Aftab Alam Khan of UK Action-Aid stated:

The past week's talks in Geneva could have done much to end injustice in world trade. But all they have achieved is to narrowly avoid the kind of deadlock which ended last year's meeting of trade ministers in Cancun, Mexico. The injustices, including the notorious US and European Union farm subsidies, remain. African farmers grow some of the world's best cotton. They can produce three kilos of cotton for the cost of one kilo grown in the US. By subsidising its 30,000 cotton farmers, the US is depressing world prices and undermining the economies of four West African countries – Benin, Burkina Faso, Mali and Togo – whose 10 million people depend on cotton for 30 to 50% of their national income. This agreement does not address the real issue, the need to eliminate all cotton subsidies. Again, the US has been let off the hook at the expense of some of the world's poorest people. The EU has also wriggled out of firm commitments in reform of its common agricultural policy. The £1.4bn the EU spends on subsidising dairy products and the £1.2bn spent on sugar will continue. How can poor farmers compete, when farmers in rich countries can sell their goods at below the cost of production? So why did developing countries agree to this bad deal? The answer is simple: the trade talks are heavily weighted in rich countries' favour. Elite groups meet in secret to make proposals poor countries are pressured to accept. Poor countries are not asking for charity; they are after justice. What they want are fair-trade rules, in which everyone shares the benefits of world trade.

Furthermore, in its editorial section, the same newspaper's caption is "Rich countries must give more if they are serious about creating a global free market". The paper identified the three major issues as agriculture, industrial goods and customs procedures, and concluded by saying that the time when there is one law for the rich and another for the poor is running out. Prior to the subsidies, there existed the Multi-Fibre Agreement (MFA). Under the MFA, the developed countries put quotas on the import of textiles and apparel in order to protect their own employment-intensive textile industries. As with raw cotton (even though the MFA has been abolished), the Western textile industry remains heavily protected through both tariffs and quotas. In short, agricultural subsidies still remain very high. Each EU cow farmer receives a subsidy every day. Each EU wheat farmer derives half of his income from subsidies. What about the poor coffee farmers in Kenya and Rwanda? They produce crops that are supposed to give them and the farm labourers they employ money for food, shelter, children's education, medicine and clothes. Even when they are not fighting the vagaries of nature, such as droughts, they are fighting the world coffee prices that are sometimes artificially lowered through subsidies. On these products alone, the supermarkets in the West would be declaring millions of pounds in profit each year; yet the farmers in Africa barely survive from producing these goods. So how can developing countries compete?

On 1 June 2005 The Independent analysed the problem, and in addition, gave solutions as follows:

TRADE

1985 – Unfair trade practices, tariff barriers and agricultural subsidies have long been blamed for Africa's underdevelopment. Trade barriers and agricultural subsidies in the West affect exports such as cotton, peanuts or groundnuts, tobacco and beef. Côte d'Ivoire, Mauritius and South Africa export manufactured goods which encounter trade barriers in the West.

2005 – Tony Blair has pointed out that the European Union's farm subsidies are a disaster for Africa. Farming accounts for some 70% of employment on that continent, but most of the farmers there are desperately poor. Subsidised products dumped on their markets by exporters from the United

States and the EU unfairly undercut their prices. But the underlying problem is that the rich nations set the global trade rules.

SOLUTION

Urgent action is needed to scrap trade-distorting subsidies paid to farmers in the developed world, and allow the creation of a level playing field. In some of the most impoverished African nations, fewer than half of the children are in primary school, and fewer still go to secondary school. The UN has devised a cure for such economic stagnation, which includes a massive rise in direct financial aid – something the G8 has yet to support.

DEMOCRACY

1985 – From the diamonds which Emperor Bokassa of the Central African Republic gave to the then French President, Valery Giscard d'Estaing, to the antics of the late Sani Abacha who ran Nigeria from 1993 to 1998, corruption has been endemic in many African regimes. More than £1.5bn of Abacha's and other Nigerian leaders' ill-gotten gains turned up in British banks, only a fraction of which ever made it back to Nigeria.

2005 – Human rights are under threat across Africa, from the practice of female genital mutilation to the arbitrary arrests of opposition politicians and human rights workers. In Zimbabwe, opposition MPs have been beaten and activists tortured, and in Congo thousands have been killed in ethnic conflicts. Impoverishment and impunity have fuelled a pattern of extreme violence in countries such as Liberia, Sierra Leone and Côte d'Ivoire.

SOLUTION

Democracy, the UN says, is the only political arrangement that guarantees political and civil freedom. In addition, it helps to protect people from economic and political catastrophes such as famine. The Africa Commission report calls for rich countries, and particularly their financial services industries to do more to fight corruption. African leaders also need to root out corruption and promote good governance.

As for the newspaper's proposed solutions, the suggested remedy for subsidies is quite right, but let's not fool ourselves; the UN has yet to come up with a lasting solution for African economic stagnation. On the issue of democracy and corruption, the newspaper diagnosed the problems well, but was not able to suggest a more serious solution such as involving the UN in the conduct of elections rather than mere monitoring. In terms of corruption in a place like Nigeria, the paper was right when it said that Nigerian leaders' ill-gotten monies turn up in British banks. But the paper failed to suggest solutions to this. It is unfortunate that when a hardworking British resident goes along to any UK bank with £10,000 in cash, the bank wants to know how the person got the money. But when a million pounds in cash from Nigeria appears at the same bank, there will not be any such question. Similarly, a hardworking UK resident buys a house by obtaining a mortgage, but when a Nigerian leader arrives in Europe with a million pounds to buy a house, no one remembers money-laundering. What about the foreign oil companies lobbying to get oil contracts? The pressure groups want oil companies to be publishing all payments made to oil producing countries such as Nigeria, as this will help to limit corruption. It requires an international regulation that makes such disclosures mandatory.

Paradoxically, the developing countries have been compelled to borrow from leading institutions such as the IMF in order to meet their external debt obligations and for infrastructure development. Some of them seek to reschedule their debts. Whether they are looking to reschedule or looking for a new loan, the developing countries must submit a structural adjustment programme to the IMF for approval. One of the important elements of the IMF conditionality is the removal of barriers to international trade. This means that small-scale industries in developing countries that are producing primarily for the domestic market and behind protectionist barriers can no longer develop and expand their operations. Assuming the country is one of the least developed countries with a small domestic market, it is logical that manufacturing should be labour-intensive and concentrated on simple mechanical processes that use local materials and produce non-durable consumer products, such as clothing and food. For more advanced developing countries such as Nigeria, Brazil and Indonesia with large domestic markets, a combination of labour-intensive and capital-intensive technologies might be appropriate. They can produce intermediate consumer goods and capital goods for both internal and regional markets. However, pursuing capital-intensive strategies may lead to some bottlenecks, such as:

- Certain activities of the large foreign capital-intensive industries, such as effective promotion and advertisement may cripple or lead to the extinction of local indigenous industries.

- Due to fear of losing markets and low quality semi-finished products, large-scale modern industries do not favour inter-industry links with the domestic industries; instead, they import from their associates abroad.
- Production disruptions could occur as a result of lack of foreign exchange.
- As modern capital-intensive industries create large production outputs, the country has to remove some import restriction in order to export into international markets. This will heavily expose the economy to the international market, thereby crippling some infant industries.

All this said, much will depend on the WTO promise to eliminate all forms of export subsidies by the end of 2013.

Other things that the countries adopting import-substitution industrialization should do, include: grant tax holidays to newly formed industries; establish industrial estates at subsidized rents; and provide necessary services and adequate infrastructure within these areas. Of course, the benefits of all these are that domestic natural resources will be utilized more and local job opportunities will be created.

Export-Led Industrialization

In the preceding paragraphs, the discussion has been centred on import-substitution industrialization. This is usually the first step, but the next step involves the gradual progression through successive stages of comparative advantage utilization into export-led industrialization. To treat developing countries' export-led industrialization properly, they should be classed into two different categories: the small least-developed countries, and the larger developing countries. The small least-developed countries consist of those with meagre natural resources, agriculture as the main productive activity, small internal markets and lacking the technological and infrastructural prerequisites for industrialization. By contrast, the large developing countries comprise those that have started industrial production based on their natural resources, have sizeable internal markets, rely on cheap labour and may have started to export in large quantities. Although countries like Singapore and Hong Kong have small populations, they do not fit into the first category because they have already leapfrogged to semi-advanced nation status. However, for the purposes of illustration, Singapore and Hong Kong will be classed as large developing countries, while countries in the first category will include Benin, Burkina Faso, Mali and Togo. Although Singapore and Hong Kong's strategies have worked for them, small nations will have to be very careful in adopting their own development strategies for the following reasons:

- The export of agricultural products may create food shortages locally.
- The international market is volatile; as such, penetration may be difficult.
- It may only be possible to set up "screwdriver" plants because most materials and components will be imported from abroad. But will these meet the local content requirements?
- Lack of technological capabilities will hamper capital-intensive production.
- Due to their small populations, they do not have much bargaining power to negotiate on trade liberalization or penetration with other countries.
- Although the WTO members have reaffirmed their commitment to helping small economies become fully integrated in the world trading system, one is yet to see this happen. After all, the Uruguay Round GATT negotiation made a similar commitment but was not able to accomplish it.

Let us look at the export-led industrialization strategy in large developing countries. Many countries in this category have taken export-led options and succeeded. Typical examples are Taiwan, Hong Kong, Singapore, Malaysia, Brazil and the Republic of Korea. Others such as Nigeria, South Africa, India, Indonesia and Kenya may follow. Before we go into the choice of technologies, let's look at what is required for the export-led strategy to take off:

- o Protectionism and international politics
- o Local content requirement
- o Export processing zones
- o Export tax and sales incentives
- o Export cartels
- o Export credits
- o Export quality inspection
- o Export marketing
- o Export awards

Protectionism and International Politics

Using the Common Agricultural Policy (CAP), the EU's trade and protectionist policies discriminate against developing countries. For example, each EU cow farmer receives an average annual net subsidy of $2.50. However, the compromise deal inked at the WTO in 2005 between developed nations and developing countries was for the developed countries to cut subsidies for farmers in exchange for an agreement by developing countries to open up their markets by cutting tariffs and reducing customs procedures. The cost of cutting tariffs falls mainly on the large developing countries that are expected to be or will be exporting semi-finished and finished goods to the rich nations. It means import duties have to be reduced in such a way that the highest are cut the most. Following that, developing countries are also expected to negotiate on rules to make customs procedures in their countries easier and less expensive for importers. This will make imported goods from developed countries cheaper, and as such, local consumers will prefer foreign goods to locally manufactured ones. This may therefore lead to the extinction of infant industries and increased unemployment rates in the developing countries. Alternatively, the cutting of tariffs could be considered differently. Depending on the chosen sector to be given high priority for expansion, one could place fewer tariffs in some sectors and more in others. Whether this method will be accepted by the WTO is another question. In Taiwan, the method is that the higher the proportion of imports used as inputs into further production, the lower the non-tariff barriers (NTB). Taiwan has higher tariffs on final goods than on raw materials.

As we have seen previously, there are three highly divisive subjects in the WTO negotiations: agricultural subsidies, the opening of markets and customs procedures. It is assumed that any time a deal is closed, the developing countries will be the main losers. This is because they have to open their markets more and reduce the burden of customs, making the goods from developed countries very cheap, which in turn will lead to Western goods being dumped in their countries. It is obvious that some developed countries have no sympathy whatsoever for the developing countries. They give them aid with one hand and take it back with the other. Rich countries must give more if they are serious about creating a global free market. They must help all the developing countries to nurture and protect their infant industries. Almost all the developed countries went through stages of protectionist policies before the capabilities of their firms reached the point where a policy of free trade was declared to be in the national interest. Britain was protectionist when it was trying to catch up with Holland. Germany was protectionist when it was trying to catch up with Britain. The US was protectionist when it was trying to catch up with Britain and Germany. Japan was protectionist for most of the twentieth century, right up to the 1970s, and Korea and Taiwan up to the 1990s, but none of them came close to matching the criteria for "democracy" until the very late stages of their development.

Preventing the developing countries from catching up first became an issue during the Bretton Woods Conference in 1944. The theme of the conference was centred on the management of the post-war international economy. At that time there was anticipation that decolonization would occur. The North knew that the southern nationalist leaders were concerned with how to pursue economic independence. They knew that the economic independence of the South meant economic protectionism. The Western leaders were aware of the political consequences, such as high unemployment rates and the impact it could have on their own countries. Then, knowing that southern leaders would need money to carry out projects in their respective countries, the northern leaders created two multilateral organizations (the IMF, and the World Bank or International Bank for Reconstruction and Development (IBRD)). The IMF (International Monetary Fund) was to supply states with money to help them overcome short-term balance of payment difficulties. But such money is only made available after the borrowing country has agreed to implement a structural adjustment programme (SAP), which usually includes the lifting of import barriers for goods from the North. The World Bank finances projects such as roads, schools and power plants, but the recipient nations have to agree to certain policy reforms too. In many nations, the structural adjustment programmes have exacerbated the level of poverty by creating a net outflow of wealth from these nations. Theoretically, these organizations are UN agencies but, unlike other arms of the UN, they are not accountable to the UN General Assembly, where the rule of "one state, one vote" operates. Instead, the World Bank and IMF answer to their major shareholders, which are the governments of the North (Raffer and Singer, 2001). These organizations burden the borrowers with conditions that are favourable to the North's economy. One of the major conditions is the "liberalization" of the borrower's economy. The World Bank and IMF use economic liberalism to ensure that the South cannot protect its infant industries; hence, the goods of the

North can continue to be dumped into the territories of the South. Writing decades ago, Friedrich List observed:

It is a very clever common device that when anyone has attained the summit of greatness, he kicks away the ladder by which he has climbed up, in order to deprive others of the means of climbing up after him. Any nation which by means of protective duties and restrictions on navigation has raised her manufacturing power and has navigation to such a degree of development that no nation can sustain free competition with her, can do nothing wiser than to throw away these ladders of her greatness, to preach to other nations the benefits of free trade, and to declare in penitent tones that she has hitherto wandered in the paths of error, and has now for the first time succeeded in discovering the truth (List, 1966 (1885): 368).

However, how a developing country is adversely affected by or favourably benefits from these external influences partly depends on its negotiating power. If its negotiators or leaders are not bribed or co-opted by the developed countries' own negotiators, they can negotiate themselves into the international market.

Local Content Requirement

The local content requirement prescribes the minimum percentage of domestic input (e.g. materials, components and manpower) to be included in any manufacturing process, in order to ensure or promote the utilization of local resources and fuller integration of foreign investments in the national economy. It has been used to foster backward linkages in a number of sectors, such as automobile plants, televisions, air conditioners and refrigerators. It is an essential condition in direct foreign investment agreements. In some cases, such local content requirements are preconditions for giving investment incentives. Such requirements must be stipulated in all regional economic plans; absent that, the regional free market will be abused by the multinational corporations. A typical example is the case of France and the imposition of restrictions on Nissan cars exported there from the United Kingdom in the 1980s (despite laws guaranteeing the free movement of goods within the European Community), on the basis of insufficient European local content or value added in the UK.

Case Study 1: Local Content Requirement

The case of Nissan in Europe (as with other Japanese automobile manufacturers establishing assembly plants abroad) represents a classic example of foreign investment to protect export shares in response to protectionist actions or threats. A major concern of the host country in such situations is to ensure that the investment is not a mere "screwdriver factory", which only assembles imported components in order to avoid import restrictions on the finished products. This concern lies behind the imposition of a local content or value-added requirement. The decision of the French government (effective in 1989) to include Nissan Bluebird cars imported from the Nissan plant in Sunderland, United Kingdom in Nissan French import quota – thereby treating them as Japanese exports – was on the basis of insufficient local content added in the United Kingdom. At the time the dispute arose, the local (UK) content of the cars was calculated at 70% and was expected to reach 80% by the end of 1989, whereas France (and Italy as well) required 80% minimum local content, below which the car was considered of non-European origin and subject to import quotas. The controversy over those import restraints became part of a general debate over the European Community's strategy to restore the competitiveness of the European automobile industry after 1992, a debate which was yet to be concluded but which contemplated the possibility of replacing national import quotas with global community quotas or negotiating "voluntary" export restraints on Japanese cars (UNCTC, 1990).

Although some form of local content requirement is necessary, developing countries should insist on percentages that are reasonably competitive and, if possible, a uniform percentage should apply across a regional economic union or continent. It is also very important that in order to maximize the contribution of the local content regime, the ancillary industries that lead to backward integration of the main production line be encouraged. Let us look at the synopsis of such mistakes that were made in the case of Nigeria's quest for industrialization, as stated by Aliyu:

"A summation of the critical issues identified in the course of appraising the performance of the manufacturing sub-sector points to an obvious fact, which is the low level of production in the past two decades by the manufacturing sector. Furthermore, the industrialization strategy adopted was simply analogous to someone trying to climb a tree from its top. Simple examples include the establishment of steel production plants without the establishment of iron ore concentrate, formed coke, lime and alloys beneficiating plants; the establishment of fertilizer factories without the establishment of the phosphate beneficiating plants, potash processing, sulphuric acid and phosphate acid plants. Also, the establishment of motor vehicle assembly plants without the establishment of industries to produce up to 10% of the components required; the establishment of paper-producing industries without the establishment of industries to produce short/long pulp and some essential chemicals. Equally worthy of mentioning is the establishment of salt processing industries that wholly depend on imported crude salt; and the desire to produce a Nigerian made car without a corresponding effort at indigenising the technology for production of a simple bicycle" (Aliyu, 1995: 48).

The foreign investors or partners may not be interested if the host developing country has not got or is not committed to getting the necessary ancillary industries together with infrastructural facilities and is insisting on a high rate of local content requirement.

Export-Processing Zones

An export-processing zone (EPZ) is an area designated by the government for the benefit of export-oriented organizations. The companies that establish and produce within the area enjoy duty- and tax-free imported inputs, good infrastructure facilities and simplified administrative procedures for trade and remittances. The major beneficiaries are the multinational corporations whose manufacturing, or rather assembly, activities for export are mainly located in the EPZs. In Malaysia, for example, much of the increase in manufactured exports is traceable to the establishment of EPZs since the early 1970s. In fact, major production of electronics and textiles originated from the EPZs and was carried out by the multinationals. Such concentrations of multinational corporations in the zones led to the setting up of many ancillary and supporting industries there. In Taiwan, EPZs accounted for about 10% of Taiwan's export trade throughout the 1970s and 1980s. In summary, the establishment of EPZs in many developing countries will bring a new phase to the global relocation (globalization) of industries from industrialized nations and could trigger increases in exports.

Export Taxes and Sales Incentives

Export taxes may be exempted, or companies might claim rebates on all taxes paid on imports used for export inputs. Export sales are also exempted from business taxes, the import of raw materials and components for export production may be liberalized, and export credits may be given to exporters.

This form of incentive to exporters goes back to the Middle Ages, when a European government gave exporters "bounty" in the form of cash. If you were a manufacturer of shoes and received from your government a sum of money for every dozen pairs of shoes you exported, you would definitely try to manufacture more shoes for export. Manufacturers of other products would also feel the same; hence, government bounties on export were designed to promote production. Today, we have similar incentives, not only on exports but also as agricultural subsidies.

Export Cartels

To avoid cut-throat competition in the domestic market for export sales, many governments encourage their exporters to form cartels in order to regulate output and stimulate exports, and this has been happening in developed nations as well as the newly industrializing Asian countries. For example, a Taiwanese government official source stated as follows:

Unorganized production and export often lead to excessive production and cutthroat competition in foreign markets, which inevitably cause a sharp decline in price, deterioration in quality, and finally a loss of the export market. To combat these shortcomings, the Government has encouraged unified and joint marketing of exports in foreign markets through limitation of production by means of export quotas, improvement of quality and unified quotation of export prices (Fong, 1968: 415).

Similarly, the present joint stock company was first initiated in the Middle Ages following the fear of trading in unknown and considerably distant lands with strangers and under unfamiliar conditions. The old separate individual traders could not do what many individuals could who were united into a single body and acting as a unit with single management. Although the main reason for the joint stock company was to raise capital, it did also help to monopolize trade by keeping outsiders out. Since then, country after country, and sector after sector, has formed cartels in order to control a reasonable share of the international market. However, it is important to note here that cartels within a country, which are used to fix prices and limit the supply of essential commodities or other cartel-related agreements, are usually committing criminal offences. Companies or individuals engaged in such activities must be punished. This is quite different from the export cartel.

Export Credits

Under the export credit scheme, companies receive concessional credits according to their previous year's export performance and their planned exports for the current year. For example, the government of Taiwan began supplying low-cost export credits as early as 1957. When the concessional interest rate was 11.9%, the nominal bank rate for a non-export loan was 19.8% (secured) and 22.3% (unsecured). Indeed, for the period between 1966 and 1981 (with one exception), the real interest rate on export loans in South Korea was negative. This helped the exporters to be more competitive in international markets.

Export Quality Inspections

Most foreign buyers judge a product by its origin. Others, however, consider the product's brand name. Therefore, the shoddy quality of a single product can affect the reputation of producers of other products from that country. As a result, some governments make compulsory inspections of certain export items to ensure that the products meet national standards. However, because of the amount of work required to undertake product inspection, the company's quality control procedures are examined instead. Some firms are inspected once, others two or three times a year.

Export Marketing

Governments should help with export marketing. Having a Commercial Attaché in their embassies abroad is a starting point. The Commercial Attaché should be able to provide details of home products and manufacturers to importers in his host country. This person should be able to organize seminars/workshops on trade and investment opportunities in their home country. The commercial section in the embassy should undertake market research, some organized by commodity, the rest by area. As well as looking at macro issues of economic relations with other countries, the government could arrange to give technical assistance to local firms on how to design their catalogues for international buyers. However, in view of the volatile nature of foreign markets and protectionist sentiments, it may be difficult to penetrate the networked markets of the developed countries. The best way to do this is to engage the transnational corporations, for they have already established network marketing all over the globe. This is discussed more fully under the "Buyer-Driven Chains" topic below.

Export Awards

National prizes are awarded to exporters based on their volume of exports during the previous year. Such awards go back to time immemorial. In Chapter One, we saw how Queen Elizabeth I of England knighted John Hawkins for his successful slave trade expedition in the sixteenth century. The recipients of such national trophies are usually happy and it motivates them to export more. Usually, their trophies are displayed at the company headquarters. Besides, a national award gives recipients an edge over their rivals and attracts more business for them.

Choice of Industry

The choice of technology depends on whether the government of the local or regional economy wants export-oriented production or labour-intensive industrialization. The kind of trade regime and choice of product can determine the type of technology a government adopts. For an export trade regime, this means the country or local area has to compete at international level – particularly in the markets of the more developed countries. It is therefore important to consider the most recent and most appropriate technology, but this may be capital-intensive. For a technology that uses the local area's relatively abundant factors such as labour and raw materials, they may consider the best labour-intensive technology, which is ideal for import-substitution industrialization.

Cottage Industries

A speech made by the Mayor of Bradford, England in October 1853, in the presence of textile workers, reads as follows:

Instead of the manufacture being confined to the cottages, they had built palaces of industry equal to the palaces of the Caesars; instead of hand labour, they had, to the utmost, availed themselves of the almost miraculous resources of mechanical science; instead of a master manufacturer carrying a week's production upon his own back, he harnessed the iron horse to the railway train, and daily conveyed away their goods by ton (The Illustrated London News 1853).

He was reminding the workers of the changes that had taken place during their time. This was 146 years ago. How can any government in the world today place emphasis on cottage industries that prevailed in the first half of the nineteenth century in Europe? Cottage industries are sometimes called "appropriate technologies" or "traditional industries". The cottage industries are those which existed in the poor countries prior to moderniza-tion and contact with the outside world. They include simple metalworking, woodwork, bicycle repair, block moulding, carpentry and handloom weav-ing. With or without government intervention, these cottage industries will exist in every rural area. They are essential, but there do not need to be many in each village. They do not produce enough surpluses to increase labour or lead any country to rapid economic growth.

How can one compare a one-man photo laboratory that is using old black-and-white equipment with a photo lab using sophisticated QSS colour printing equipment and employing twenty staff? The first one is a cottage industry, while the second is a SMI. What people need is an industry that will create employment opportunities and provide them with skills.

A number of policy failures have taken place in the developing coun-tries. Call it micro finance or a soft loan, it has been given to many so-called cottages in some countries, and the results are usually the same. People or

85

cottages are unable to pay back the loan. How can they pay it back when they have not made sales or realized revenues with which to do so? The villagers have no money and cannot buy their surplus goods and services. Instead, the villagers want industries that will create employment opportunities for them. Because the cottage industries do not require large amounts of capital, their output is usually small, and because the quantities are small, the cost per unit of output will be high. If goods are to be transported to the cities for sale, this will increase the cost and may result in a loss. This means that those cottage industries given loans will not be able to pay them back. Sometimes, the policymakers in developing countries do not give careful consideration to the feasibility and viability of a project before embarking on it. Another policy failure, they would say. Cottage industries do not require the international transfer of technology, but neither do they contribute to industrialization, and therefore are not within the scope of this book.

Small- and Medium-Sized Industries (SMIs) vs. Large-Scale Industries

I have always supported what Schumacher calls "intermediate" technology. It is a simplified technology midway between traditional industries and the modern automated production lines. It makes use of local natural resources and creates employment opportunities, yet is not as expensive as capital-intensive technology. The ratios of labour per unit of capital and labour per unit of input are both high. The word "intermediate" may sound second best, but this is the best technology for most developing countries.

As for large-scale industries, automated technology will be ideal. It will enable the country to produce for export markets. It presupposes an easily accessible and sufficiently large market for the items produced, but in many developing countries, particularly the small ones, no such market exists. It also presupposes that there is a high level of technical capability in the host developing countries, but most often there are operational problems and deficiencies in the organization and management of production. It is also necessary to note that modern, large-scale industries can only function properly if there is a steady and reliable infrastructure development such as communications, transport, water and light. The medium-sized industry may operate, say, a generator for its light and power but the generator capacity required for a modern automated industry may be too expensive. The automated nature of the technology means fewer employment opportunities, but it does not mean that all large-scale industries are automated. A few Foreign Direct Investment (FDI) corporations such as those having a vehicle assembly plant, for example, ANAMCO in Enugu, Nigeria, are not fully automated. Although initially, ANAMCO was a "screwdriver" factory receiving all its components and materials from Germany, it was still employing a large workforce. Gradually, ANAMCO started using local raw materials and increased the local content of its final output.

In view of the foregoing discussion on some of the severe limitations of cottage industries and large-scale automated industries, it comes as no surprise that this chapter will be centred on small- and medium-sized industries (SMIs), which, in most cases, are modern and use labour-intensive technologies. It has also been proved that with economies of agglomeration and local joint action, small- and medium-sized industries can compete alongside large firms and in global markets (Schmitz, 1995). Keith Marsden of the ILO prefers the more comprehensive term progressive technologies, because it shows the dynamic elements ideal for developing countries, and he comments as follows:

They should stimulate economic progress by making optimum use of available resources. They should be conducive to social progress by enabling the mass of the population to share the benefits and not just a privileged few. They should represent technical progress, measured by improvements over existing methods and not by reference to external standards which may be inadequate. And they should be progressive in a temporal sense, i.e. their characteristics will change over time in response to the society's ability to pay for them and capacity to employ them effectively. In other words, the concept is dynamic, not static (Schmitz, 1995).

SMIs will enable developing countries to build up their technological bases and increase not only their manpower skills but also their organizational ability.

Resource-Based Industries

Development of resource-based industries (RBIs) will lead to a maximization of the efficient utilization of the country's natural resources. The industrialization process could be productively linked to the development of the mineral and agricultural sector as the main supplier of inputs into manufacturing. In other words, there will be "backward linkages" and possibly "forward linkages" in the system. These inter-industry linkages will ensure that the natural resource potential is fully developed to exploit the country's comparative advantages. Firstly, the main RBI to be promoted has to be identified. Secondly, the investors, both local and foreign, have to be found. Tables 3 and 4 below show some resource availabilities and industrial possibilities.

Table 3: Resource Availabilities vs. Industrial Possibilities

Resource Availabilities	Industrial Possibilities
Crude petroleum	Used to produce oil, propylene, gases, fuel, olefin products
Natural gas	Used to produce oil, gas, insecticides, dyes, pigments, olefins, etc.
Limestone	Cement, lime, fluxing, stone, etc.
Phosphate	Fertilizers and phosphoric acid
Sulphur	Sulphuric acid, insecticides, paper, rubber and plastic
Iron ore	Steel manufacture, nickel, manganese

Table 4: Agricultural Resources vs. Industrial Possibilities

Agricultural Resources	Industrial Possibilities
Maize, rice, wheat, millet, etc.	Cereal
Orange, grape, lemon, plantain, banana, mango, pineapple, etc.	Fruit juice
Tomato, pepper, onion, melon, waterleaf, etc.	Vegetable juice
Cotton, sugarcane, ginger, tea, cocoa, coffee, etc.	Industrial mills
Rabbit, poultry, cattle, goats, sheep, etc.	Livestock industry
Fish, shrimp, crabs, seaweeds, etc.	Sea product canning
Palm oil, kernel, and palm_olien	Various industries
Cassava, plantain, yam, etc.	Various industries
Gum, gum Arabic	Various industries

The tables are hardly exhaustive, and list just a few possibilities. Countless resources and possibilities exist, and not only with respect to the inputs necessary to produce certain products, but they are also a chance to develop by-products. A typical example is the by-product of rice or wheat called "straw". Straw can be used to make paper, particularly where timber is scarce. The industrial planners should link as many industrial capacities as possible to the raw materials that can be found in the locality. Whether they pursue import-substitution or export-led industrialization, resource-based industrialization can help. But where the country or local government does not have enough financial resources or investors, the establishment of multi-local industrial enterprises can be considered.

Multi-Local Industrial Enterprises

It is obvious that in many developing countries, the private sector is unable to promote big projects due to the huge capital investments required and the complicated nature of the technology involved. At the same time, in view of the resource constraints faced by individual governments, such as the magnitude of capital for investment; human resources in terms of management expertise and skilled manpower; the size of the market for the product; and foreign technology and knowhow, it is necessary that countries, states or local authorities in developing countries consider teaming up together in order to develop some core industries. Multi-local industrial enterprises are projects involving a number of local authorities, states or countries. Cooperation can take the form of access to members' markets, equity participation, sharing sponsorship responsibilities for promoting the development of the project, management support, and so on. The core industries may include petrochemical, metallurgical, agro-related, chemical and engineering industries, or even consumer products. These industries often provide effective linkages to other sectors of the economy, and such a strategy will help to accelerate the pace of economic development and reverse the current downward trend. It will be an important breakthrough for the region, although the success of the project will depend on the relative skills of the partners, cultural orientation, their markets and financial strengths, as well as the novelty of their development.

Major core industries can be identified as follows:
o   Building materials and construction industries;
o   Food and agro-based industries;
o   Chemical industries – pharmaceutical, fertilizer, pesticides;
o   Forest-based and textile industries;
o   Metallurgical and engineering industries, producing spare
       parts, tools, machinery, etc.;
o   Energy and energy-related industries;
o   Motor vehicle and bicycle assembling plants, etc.

To increase employment and outputs using local resources and to properly distribute income among the people and improve their quality of life, the group must not shy away from using foreign technology. Rather, what they should be concerned with is how to carry out the technology selection, negotiation and adaptation processes. Imported technology may directly affect the economic development of the recipient countries in three interrelated ways:

- Foreign technology may contribute to the local economy by exploiting existing resources, using them to generate new job opportunities for previously unemployed labour and to decrease idle capacity that has not been utilized by indigenous entrepreneurs due to their limited technical capabilities.
- Technology transfer may increase the physical stock of productive factors such as expatriate personnel, rendering technical services and impacting on or transferring their skills to local personnel. It will also bring about an increase in the local stock of machinery and foreign raw materials. But agreement with foreign technology suppliers must include the exploration of local raw materials within a specified timeframe.
- Technology transfer could lead to the productivity growth of existing factors such as labour, capital, land and other natural resources.

On the other hand, according to the United Nations Industrial Development Organization (UNIDO), the problems to be taken into account when considering the acquisition of technology for such complex industrial enterprises include:

1. The suitability of the technology in terms of marketing size; if for a smaller capacity, the plant should be modified;
2. The terms and conditions governing the acquisition of technology including the industrial property rights, i.e. patents, knowhow, trademarks and trade names, owned or licensed by the foreign partner, which affects the products to be produced by the multi-local industrial enterprise; and relevant licences granted by the foreign partner to third parties, their dates of expiration, geographical area(s) covered, conditions under which they can be terminated by the foreign partners, the products and industrial property included in each licence, and the royalties payable under each licence;
3. Whether the foreign technical partner has the management skills needed to assist the multi-local industrial enterprise it is partnering to develop an efficient and effective local management and, in addition, upgrade the technical competence of the multi-local industrial enterprise so that it can master the technology within the specified period; and

4. The cost and financial terms and conditions of acquiring the technology.

To enquire about the suitability of foreign technology for a proposed project, the project sponsors need expert advice on sources of appropriate technology. Some international institutions such as UNIDO may have relevant information on those manufacturers of industrial technologies that are willing to transfer their technologies to developing countries. Private consultants can, in addition, research and compare global technologies. It is important to shop around before making a commitment to any one technology supplier.

The project cycle is the period of identification, formulation, appraisal, implementation and monitoring of industrial projects. At the identification stage, project ideas are developed from a number of sources. These include statistical data on trade, natural resources and technology. For instance, market trends in imports and exports, economic survey reports including sector studies, suggestions from experts in particular fields and special information obtained through contacts are collected at this stage. Also at this stage, important things to consider include the objectives of the project, the expected end results and the profit levels. Other essential features, according to UNIDO, include:

1. The type of technology;
2. The type of raw materials and their availability;
3. Orientation of production, i.e. for local consumption or for export; and
4. An estimate of the total project costs.

The formation stage involves consideration of the project's economic and financial viability as well as technical feasibility. A good and positive result on these will enable the sponsors to secure financing for the project. It is also necessary to estimate the social benefits of the project at this stage. The last stage will involve a detailed analysis of the capital, management and workforce requirements of the project, as well as its projected cash flows, operation costs, socio-economic benefits and profitability.

At the implementation stage, the project sponsors carry out all necessary preparatory arrangements for project operation. These include the following activities:

• The mobilization of the necessary funds (equity and loan capital);

- Recruitment of qualified and suitable management personnel;
- Appointment of technical partners;
- Appointment of architects, surveyors, engineers and contractors for the construction of the building and infrastructure required;
- Negotiation of appropriate technology;
- Arrangement for procurement of plant, machinery and raw materials;
- Arrangement for the efficient marketing of the product; and
- Satisfactory conclusion of any other matters, e.g. obtaining import licences where necessary, which will contribute to the successful completion of the project, the initial production and the marketing of the products.

Finally, before the commissioning of the project's operation, an independent team of experts could be called in to monitor and evaluate the implementation of the project. Evaluation and monitoring should also be seen as a continuous process during the lifetime of the project. Obviously, there are many more issues which the multi-local industrial enterprise sponsors have to deal with before such a project is born. Such issues include the entities participating in the projects reaching an agreement on:

- o marketing arrangements
- o financial arrangements
- o management arrangements
- o technology acquisition arrangements
- o legal considerations
- o technical considerations
- o commercial considerations
- o monitoring and support services

Marketing Products from Multi-Local Industrial Enterprises:

Buyer-Driven Chains

Large retailers, brand-named merchandisers and trading companies play the central role in shaping decentralized production networks in a variety of exporting countries, frequently located on the periphery. This pattern of industrialization is typical in relatively labour-intensive consumer goods such as garments, footwear, toys and housewares (Gereffi et al.,

1994). A number of developing countries now engage in contract manufacturing. They produce products bought by big retail shops in developed countries. These are sometimes called Global Buyers, and that means globalization of the product market. The local enterprise signs contracts with the foreign buyers, which assures them of global market penetration. Recently, the globalization of such markets has intensified competition for producers in some countries and sectors. Let us look at global buyers in footwear from the US and UK in 1998, buying from countries like China, India, Brazil and Italy.

Table 5: Footwear Imports of the US and UK from China, India, Brazil and Italy

Producer country	US imports		UK imports	
	%	Ranking	%	Ranking
China	46.2	1	5.6	4
India	1.1	10	4.9	6
Brazil	12.0	2	5.5	5
Italy	11.5	3	26.0	1

Note: Data refer to the value of leather footwear. Trade policy has a downward effect on UK imports from China due to EU quotas, and an upward effect on US imports due to China's Most Favoured Nation status.
Source: Institute of Development Studies, 1999

Given the fact that more developing countries are now engaging in contract manufacturing for a decreasing number of global buyers, the policy makers from the multi-local industrial enterprises should learn from the global buyers what factors facilitate or constrain their buying patterns. Global buyers source from producers all over the world, and that gives them an unrivalled ability to compare which producers are the cheapest, fastest or provide the best quality.

In conclusion, there are two major questions that need to be answered in choosing a technological pathway, namely:

- Whether this pattern of industrialization is likely to lead to domestic technological autonomy; and
- To what extent the chosen pattern will ensure the provision of basic needs for the majority of the population.

Other important questions relate to the formulation of the strategic approach of technology choice, as well as the immediate decision of relevant action, such as:

- What is required from the outside;
- How to acquire it at a minimal cost;
- How to link it up with internal technological development and several raw materials.

CHAPTER FOUR
Capital for Industrial Development

Capital formation and allocation is the engine of development, but raising and investing capital is not usually a straightforward process. This is because allocation is usually done through a planning, budgetary and capital investment system. Plans, capital appropriations and project proposals are prepared at the operational levels while decisions are made at the higher levels. Any project proposal takes into consideration the available market data, sales projections, cash flow projections, the payback period, and profitability analysis. The results of this information, as well as the social impact, can determine whether or not a project is acceptable by the higher level. If accepted, then the sourcing and funding of the project starts. In this book, I shall first use the Malaysia model to demonstrate how sourcing and funding industrial development capital can be made, including the ODA, as follows:

Case Study 2: Malaysia's Raising of Capital (1987–1989)

(a) Private and Public Financial Institutions: Between 1987 and 1988, Malaysia was able to mobilize sizeable financial resources for its industrial development. One of the ways it achieved this was through a broad range of private and public sector financial institutions, namely the Central Bank (Bank Negara Malaysia), commercial banks, finance companies, insurance funds, merchant banks, development finance institutions and savings institutions. Before 1987 the Central Bank's guidelines were in place, which proved to restrict lending activities of the private banking institutions. When the guidelines expired at the end of 1987, the government imposed less restrictive lending guidelines in order to ensure the orderly supply of loans and equity to the manufacturing sector. Under these new guidelines, in 1988 the focus of the commercial banks' lending activities dramatically turned towards the manufacturing sector. For example, in 1988 $1,974 million was allocated to the manufacturing sector, compared with $159 million in 1987. This represented nearly half of the total loans extended by the commercial banks in 1988. Also, under the new guidelines a special loan fund of $300 million was set up for small-sized industries. This was applicable to loans given under a special loan scheme of the Credit Guarantee Corporation (CGC), and loans of $500 were also set aside for the Enterprise Rehabilitation Fund (ERF). The CGC is a special finance institution providing guarantees for loans to small-scale enterprises. The ERF loan was used to encourage the banks to extend assistance to ailing enterprises. Then, in 1989 a New Entrepreneurs Fund was launched and a provision of $250 million was made. The purpose was to provide funds for new ventures.

(b) Bilateral and Multilateral Assistance: Malaysia received considerable official development assistance (ODA) in the form of loans and other types of finance, and ODA doubled between 1983 and 1987. The World Bank is by far the most important multilateral institution for development assistance in Malaysia, but most of its assistance went into other sectors like agriculture, energy and education. Other assistance was provided from the Asian Development Bank (ADB) and by 1987, it had given Malaysia a cumulative amount of $1.4 billion, comprising 63 loans for 61 projects. Malaysia also received loans from the Islamic Development Bank (IDB), and between 1975 and 1987 it provided Malaysia with a total of $75 million. In addition to funding, Malaysia received technical cooperation from UNIDO and UNDP, which included:

- Policy assessment of Malaysian Industrial Policy Studies (MIPS) and the Industrial Master Plan;
- Upgrading of the Plastics Technology Centre's technical support capability;
- Sectoral projections of the manufacturing sector;
- Assistance to the Industrial Design and Packaging Centre;
- High-level advice in the establishment of a Furniture Technology Centre;
- Assistance with an Action Plan for development and promotion of industry, and generally;
- Assistance to the rubber goods industry;
- Preparatory assistance in formulating proposals to develop the ceramics industry;
- Assistance to electrical/electronics and automotive parts industries;
- Establishment of computer-assisted patent processing and
- patent information services;

- Assistance in the establishment of foundry and engineering parts industries; and
- Assistance to the Metal Industry Development Centre in disseminating advanced technology in the metal industry.

Rapid Influx of Foreign Investments

There were several factors that contributed to a rapid influx of foreign firms to Malaysia:

1) The four newly industrialized countries (Taiwan, Hong Kong, Singapore and South Korea) were not granted Preferential Duty Treatment for their goods by the United States under the Generalized System of Preferences (GSP) scheme. This encouraged these countries to locate some of their industries in Malaysia in order to reap the benefits of GSP.
2) The government's promotional incentives and investment policies were favourable to the investors. Moreover, the concept of free trade zones (FTZs) was seen as an incentive and encouraged the flow of direct foreign investment, particularly into the electronics sector.
3) Importantly, good infrastructure development was also seen by investors as an essential factor. Other factors included the relatively cheaper, young, trainable labour force, as well as inexpensive land. All of these made the investments gather momentum.

By analysing the above case study, one can see that the process of raising finance for industrial development by a non-oil producing country like Malaysia was not simple. It called for a sense of leadership that believed in asceticism and commitment towards Malaysia's quest for national industrialized status. Its efforts were successful in securing assistance and investment from the following:

- Public and private financial institutions such as the Central Bank (Bank Negara), commercial banks, merchant banks, insurance funds, savings banks and development finance institutions;

- Credit Guarantee Corporation (CGC) and Enterprise Rehabilitation Fund (ERF);

- Asian Development Bank (ADB);
- Islamic Development Bank (IDB);
- World Bank;
- United Nations Industrial Development Organization (UNIDO);
- United Nations Development Programme (UNDP);
- General System of Preferences (GSP) from USA; and in establishing government lending guidelines;
- industrial policy such as infrastructural development;
- investors' incentives such as Free Trade Zones (FTZs);
- external financial flow – the main players are the multinational corporations, whose manufacturing or assembling plants for export products were located in Malaysia's FTZs.

Small Firms' Loan Guarantee Scheme

The Small Firms' Loan Guarantee Scheme (SFLG) provides a government guarantee for loans by approved lenders in many parts of the globe. Loans are made to firms or individuals who are unable to obtain conventional finance because they lack a good track record, collateral or security. Depending on the country, the guarantee generally covers 70–85% of the outstanding loan. In some countries, the percentage is higher for well-established businesses. The United Kingdom's experience will be our case study, as follows.

Case Study 3: UK – Small Firms' Loan Guarantee Scheme

Following repeated recommendations by government committees, including the Wilson, Bolton and Macmillan Commissions, the Loan Guarantee Scheme (LGS) was established in 1981. The LGS was originally set up by the Department of Trade and Industry (DTI), was then transferred to the Department of Employment in 1985 and then back to the DTI in May 1992. The purpose of the LGS initiative was to help finance existing small firms and start-ups. The scheme was particularly intended to help an entrepreneur whose proposition to borrow up to £250,000 of capital would be acceptable to a bank but for the fact that he was unable to provide adequate security for the loan. In this case, the DTI guaranteed up to 85% of the loan, encouraging the bank to grant it. If the company failed, the DTI would reimburse the bank 85% of the loan. By March 1997 over 60,000 loans had been guaranteed at a value of more than £2 billion – some achieving notable success, for example, the bookshop Waterstones.

It is important to emphasize that the LGS is a joint venture between the DTI and the banks, and that all commercial decisions affecting the borrower are taken by the bank. The DTI simply checks the eligibility of applicants. Under "small loan arrangements", the banks can make loans of up to £30,000 without the application first being referred to the DTI.

Term: Loans are not available if normal commercial finance can be raised. If the founding directors of a company have personal assets (e.g. equity in a house), then this must be used as security for a conventional bank loan before an LGS loan can be considered. This, in turn, makes the LGS scheme particularly appropriate for young entrepreneurs who do not yet own substantial personal assets.

The LGS scheme has evolved since its introduction in 1981. For a business that has been trading for less than two years, the maximum LGS loan is £100,000 and the DTI will guarantee 70% of this. A bank may take charge of the assets of a company as security towards the loan, but is not entitled to take personal guarantees from the entrepreneurs or a charge over any of their personal assets. Personal assets should have already been used to secure conventional loans before an application is made for an LGS loan. For an established business which has been trading for more than two years, the maximum LGS loan is £250,000 and the DTI guarantees 85% of this. In exchange for its guarantee, the DTI charges a premium of 1.5% per annum on the whole loan for normal variable rate lending, or 0.5% per annum for fixed rate lending. The lending institution (normally a bank) will also charge a premium, typically 2.5% above the bank base rate, so, for example, the typical cost of an LGS loan in July 1996 was 9.25%, made up of the base rate (5.25%) plus the bank premium (2.5%) plus the DTI LGS premium (1.5%). Without the DTI's guarantee for 85% of the loan, the bank would probably charge a much higher premium over the base rate for a loan with an equivalent degree of risk, so an LGS loan is good value for the borrower. The terms of the loan agreement vary, and some include a capital repayment holiday – a period in which the borrower is not required to make repayments of the loan itself, but still has to pay the interest and premiums.

Timescale of Investments: Medium-term only, between two and ten years. Degree of Involvement: The basic terms of the loan require quarterly financial management information to be provided to the lender. This would normally include a comparison between the actual and projected cash flows, and the actual and projected profit and loss figures. The borrower also agrees to supply the DTI with a progress report if requested. Where the LGS has been made through a venture capital company such as 3i, which may also have provided an early investment, a slightly higher degree of involvement may be expected.

Eligibility: The LGS is open to many small businesses. There is an overriding limit of two hundred employees, otherwise "small" is defined as: Manufacturers having a turnover of not more than £3m in the 12 months prior to the application and all other sectors having a turnover of not more than £1.5m (Cary, 1998).

Purpose of Loan: An LGS loan can be used for business purposes only, such as the development of a project, starting up trading, expanding an existing business or improving efficiency. It cannot be used to replace an existing loan, to buy shares, to pay interest on a previous loan, or to buy out members of a partnership, but it may be used to buy the assets of a business, i.e. a total company buy-out (Cary, 1998).

Developing countries are certainly in a position to learn from the experiences of countries like the UK. The LGS is one of those lessons. One can see that in less than 16 years a total of two billion pounds worth of business loans had been guaranteed, resulting in over 60,000 loans. Essentially, this has created millions of job opportunities for residents in the UK.

Build-Today-and-Privatize-Tomorrow (BTPT)

Although the suggestion in Chapter Three is for countries, states or local authorities to team up with one another in order to establish big industries, one cannot fail to agree that many states or local authorities are so financially buoyant that they can carry out such projects on their own. The role of states in most parts of Asia, in their quest for industrialization status, is to actively participate in the business sector. Such participation has been an integral part of their growth strategies and very noticeable in China, Indonesia and Malaysia. Until recently, all businesses of a significant size in China were owned by either the central or local government. These enterprises ranged from plantations, steel plants, airlines, construction and heavy industrial machines to the exploitation of natural resources such as crude oil. In Indonesia, the nationalization of foreign industries led to the state ownership of most big industries. In Malaysia, the role of the government is very pervasive, as the government has specifically created firms so as to enable it to implement its economic policy. Typical examples are PERNAS and RENONG, and to control strategic resources they created PETRONAS. Likewise, to engage in heavy industries they established HICOM (Heavy Industries Corporation of Malaysia). In short, with the exception of Hong Kong and Japan, state participation and ownership of enterprises is very common across Asian countries, and particularly, in areas that require large investment outlays.

However, the management of these large enterprises may be problematic in some countries, and to avoid this the system of Build-Today-and-Privatize-Tomorrow (BTPT) should be given serious consideration. BTPT is a system of building industries and selling them upon completion. They can be sold to the public or to private operators. The private operators do not have the capital to build such businesses, but by buying or leasing from the government and paying the cost by installments they are able to increase economic activities in a certain area. In the 1950s the Taiwanese government established a number of upstream industries such as glass, plastics, steel and cement, which it then ran as public enterprises or instead handed the factories over to selected private entrepreneurs. It is believed that economic growth was bound to be slow unless there was an adequate supply of entrepreneurs looking for opportunities who were willing to take risks. At the same time, public enterprises dominated sectors such as fuels, chemicals, mining and metalworking, food processing, textiles, fertilizer and utilities in the 1950s to 1960s.

Elsewhere, up until the early 1970s, the state ownership of industries ruled. This is because state ownership was seen as the chief instrument for the promotion of economic growth and industrial development. But contrary to this perception, nationalized industries began making a loss, and became inefficient throughout the world. In order to keep these industries in operation, state governments continued to subsidize them. Payments such as regular subsidies to these industries have brought down many governments, as monies that were supposed to have been used to fulfill other electoral promises were used to subsidize the loss-making and inefficiency of state-owned industries. So, what sounded cutting edge in the 1960s had become a boomerang?

It is therefore no exaggeration to say that the arrival of privatization, riding on a wave of resurgent economic liberalism, has fundamentally transformed the political landscape everywhere, and has spread widely across the globe. In fact, The Economist of 22 November 1997 carried an interesting advertisement, headed "Privatization in Mongolia". It offered no fewer than 700 state companies for sale, mostly in mining, tourism, food processing and real estate, but also included the Mongolian state airline MIAT.

Because the success of privatization can be seen in many countries, it has become a necessary part of the development agenda for developing countries. It attracts foreign investment, opens the way for competition and takes away the burden of running and financing loss-making state-owned enterprises. State disengagement is also an attack on state-based corruption. Importantly, it is believed that many of these loss-making industries might show up extensive profitable opportunities in the private sector.

There are different ways in which a state may wish to carry out privatization. These include:

1. The management–worker buy-out;
2. Bid from a consortium or private firms;
3. Sale of shares to the public.

The management–worker buy-out can act as an incentive for workers of the privatized industry. Bids from a consortium or private firms can attract more foreign investors into the country, hence creating more revenue for the state to redistribute. But the share issue type of privatization is the most common. It can broaden and deepen domestic capital markets, boosting liquidity and potential economic growth. But if the capital market in such a developing country is insufficiently developed, it may be difficult to find enough buyers. In such a situation, the government may decide to have listings in the more advanced and liquid markets such as Euronext, the London Stock Exchange, or the New York or Hong Kong Stock Exchanges.

The proponents of privatization have listed the following as advantages:

- Performance: State-run industries tend to be bureaucratic. A political government may only be motivated to improve a function when its poor performance becomes politically sensitive, and such an improvement can be reversed easily by another regime.
- Improvements: Conversely, the government may put off improvements due to political sensitivity and special interests – even in cases of companies that are well run and better serve their customers' needs.
- Corruption: A monopolized area is prone to corruption; decisions are made primarily for political reasons or the personal gain of the decision-maker rather than economic ones. Also, corruption during the privatization process can result in significant under-pricing of assets. Although morally wrong, such corrupt value transfer could rescue a cash-strapped industry.
- Accountability: Managers of privately owned companies are accountable to their owners/shareholders and to the consumers. But managers of publicly owned companies are required to be more accountable to the political stakeholders. These groups can reduce the managers' ability to make effective commercial judgements and to serve the needs of their customers.
- Goals: A political government tends to run an industry for political rather than economic goals.

Although universally accepted by policymakers worldwide, there are still some concerns about privatization. For example:

(1) Will the privatized industries be able to meet certain social and non-economic obligations?
(2) Will the capital market be big enough to absorb the flotation of a large organization?
(3) Will there be competitive pressures on the privatized industries?
(4) Will the privatized industries be regulated in order to protect the interests of consumers?

These fears can be eliminated if the state parliament can clearly define the social obligations that privatized industries have to incorporate into their charters. This is achieved by the government setting up an independent watchdog for each industry. A typical example in the UK is the watchdog for gas supply. This is called Ofgas (Office of Gas and Electricity Markets).

It is an independent regulatory body set up under the Gas Act 1986. The main purposes of this Act are:

(a) To privatize British Gas;
(b) To establish Ofgas as the gas industry watchdog;
(c) To set up a Gas Consumers' Council to represent the interests of gas consumers in terms of prices and level of services;
(d) To facilitate the development of competition in the gas market.

The watchdog can police and prosecute organizations that violate their rules and regulations. With these measures, the state government will be reassured that privatizing newly built state industries will not reduce the standards or increase the prices of such services. But what happens to the monies realized from the newly privatized industries? These monies can be used to establish more industries and then privatize them soon after. The regulatory body will also help to avoid the sad experience of Zambia. Privatization there led to the sale of their local industries to foreign competitors, who immediately after acquisition shut down the plants so as to eliminate local competition. The result was that local products disappeared off the market and were replaced by better quality foreign products. This move inevitably led to increased unemployment and its negative effects.

Build-Operate-and-Transfer (BOT)

One of the challenges facing developing countries is how to efficiently access capital from the capital-exporting countries for infrastructure development. BOT is a form of project financing whereby a private entity receives a concession (usually from the government) to design, finances, construct and operate a facility as stated in the concession contract. It is a technique used to finance the building of major projects. The investor will place primary reliance on the revenues from the project for their repayment. They collect their revenue at source. The arrangement is normally long-term in nature and the costs are recovered during the concession period.

Normally, such projects provide for the infrastructure to be transferred to the government at the end of the concession period. There is no collateral requirement, as the security taken by the lender is usually confined to the project assets. The structure of BOT is usually complex, as the risks of the project are spread between the various participating parties.

Examples of countries using BOT are the Philippines, India, Malaysia, Japan and Croatia; in some countries such as Australia, New Zealand and Canada, the term used is Build-Own-Operate-Transfer (BOOT). In this book, the Philippines is used as a case study, as follows:

Case Study 4: The Philippines' BOT and the Manila Metro Rail System

Background:

The Build-Operate-and-Transfer (BOT) Centre took its roots from the issuance of Administrative Order (AO) No. 105, S. 1989 creating the Coordinating Council of the Philippines Assistance Programme (CCPAP) under the Office of the President (OP) for the overall implementation of the Philippines Assistance Programme (PAP) and then, later, the BOT Programme No. 166, S. 1993.

The passage of the BOT Law (R.A. no. 6957) in July 1990, and the Amended BOT Law (R.A. no. 7718) of May 1994, strengthened the role of the CCPAP in the coordination and monitoring of project implementation under the law. A novel legislation, the BOT Law was the cornerstone for the building of power plants by the sector that solved the perennial and debilitating power outages throughout the country in the 1990s.

CCPAP was then reorganized and converted into the Coordinating Council for Private Sector Participation (CCPSP) by virtue of Administrative Order No. 67 dated 11 May 1999, for the formulation of policies and guidelines and the coordination and monitoring of the Private Sector Participation (PSP) programme and projects of the government, including projects with ODA financing, pursued under the Amended BOT Law. Finally, with the issuance of Executive Order (EO) No. 144 in November 2002, the CCPSP was reorganized and converted into the BOT Centre. Its attachment was transferred from the Office of the President to the Department of Trade and Industry (DTI) for greater coordination in promoting investments in BOT/PSP projects, in order to accelerate and sustain economic growth. In short, the BOT Centre is mandated to promote Public–Private Partnerships (PPPs) in national and local infrastructure and development projects through the BOT Law, as well as to advocate policy initiatives in the continued evolution of the country's infrastructure privatization policy framework.

Manila Metro Rail Transit System

The Manila Metro Rail Transit System, popularly known as the MRT, Metrostar Express or Metrostar, is part of the metropolitan rail infrastructure in the Manila area of the Philippines.

The MRT is operated by the Metro Rail Transit Corporation (MRTC), a private company operating in partnership with the Philippines government. In the 1990s the MRTC was awarded a Build-Operate-and-Transfer contract by the Department of Transportation and Communication (DOTC). The DOTC would have ownership of the system and assume all administrative functions, such as the regulation of fares and operations. The MRTC would have responsibility over the construction and maintenance of the system and the procurement of spare parts for trains. In exchange, the DOTC would pay the MRTC monthly fees for a certain number of years to reimburse any costs incurred.

Construction started on 16 September 1997 after the MRTC signed an amended turnkey agreement with a consortium of companies, which included Mitsubishi Heavy Industries and Sumitomo Corporation. Local companies were subcontracted for civil works, design and technical management consultancy. During the construction, the DOTC undertook technical supervision of the project activities covered by the BOT contract, while the MRTC oversaw the design, construction, equipment, testing and commissioning. The DOTC also sought the services of Systra, a French consultancy firm, with regard to the technical competence, experience and track records of firms involved in the construction and operations. By 20 July 2000 the project was completed. Initially, the number of users was low, but by 2004 MRT had the highest number of users of all the three lines in Manila, recording a daily average of 400,000 passengers.

On 3 March 2009 the Build-Operate-and-Transfer (BOT) Centre's Executive Director, Pascual R. de Guzman, made a presentation entitled "A look at BOT – Infrastructure Projects" before Belgian and other foreign businessmen during the Philippines Business Mission Conference at the EDSA Shangri-La Hotel. He invited them to invest in several BOT projects in the pipeline after giving an overview of the BOT/Private Sector Participation (PSP) programme and the services that the BOT Centre provided. At the end of the conference there were business-matching activities, where the local businessmen met with their foreign counterparts to explore possible joint venture opportunities and partnerships in the future.

During the period 1 to 8 April 2009, a delegation of officials from the Bangladesh government attended a training programme on Infrastructure

Project Development and Management, which was organized by the Asian Institute of Development Studies Inc. (AIDS) in partnership with the BOT Centre. The objective of the programme was to explain to the Bangladeshi officials the way the BOT Centre worked to promote and develop Public–Private Partnerships (PPP) in infrastructure projects. It also facilitated an exchange of the country's experiences in PPP project identification, promotion, project development, contract monitoring, and issues and challenges that affect project implementation. The delegation also visited some PPP projects like Manila Water Services Inc. (MWSI), the National Kidney and Transplant Institute (NKTI), South Luzon Expressway (SLEX) and Southern Tagalog Arterial Road (STAR).

The Bangladesh delegation was composed of representatives from the Planning Commission, Board of Investment, Ministry of Finance, and the Bangladesh Central Bank. The purpose of describing this process here is to illustrate how developing countries can, as Bangladesh has done, learn from the experiences of other developing countries as well.

Public–Private Partnerships (PPPs) or Private Finance Initiatives (PFIs)

Due to a high level of government borrowing in the 1970s and 1980s, pressure mounted on the UK government to change its standard model of the public procurement system. The government then sought to encourage private investment in infrastructure. The Public–Private Partnership (PPP) concept was born. It describes a government service or private venture which is funded and operated through a partnership of the government and one or more private sector companies. For example, a private sector consortium forms a special company called a "Special Purpose Vehicle" (SPV) to design, build, maintain and operate the assets for the contracted period. The difference between a PPP and a BOT is that in the case of the former, the government provides capital outlay as well. The capital could be by way of tax revenues or in kind, such as the transfer of existing assets. In such cases, the government is allotted an equity share in the SPV.

A typical example of a PPP is a hospital building financed and constructed by a private developer and then leased to the hospital authority. The private developer then acts as landlord, providing housekeeping and other non-medical services, while the hospital itself provides medical services.

Obviously, this is a complex arrangement for most developing countries and can only be adopted by the well-advanced developing nations. Not only is its negotiating nature complicated, but it has also been controversial in many countries. But in Lagos State, which is one of the richest states in Nigeria, PPP programmes have been adopted and have been working very successfully. The state government has used PPP to build waste management and road infrastructure projects.

But the Private Finance Initiative (PFI), which was developed by the UK's government and is a method of providing financial support for Public–Private Partnerships (PPP) between the public and private sectors, is easier to adopt. The PFI has now been adopted in many developed countries and remains the UK government's preferred method for public sector procurement.

How it works is that a public sector authority signs a contract with a private sector consortium, technically known as a Special Purpose Vehicle, as we saw in PPP. Again, the success of this venture depends on a number of variables, including the country's social virtues, which were discussed in Chapter Two. Therefore, only the well-advanced developing countries are encouraged to engage in PFI.

Two-Step Loans or Bank-to-Bank Loans

With this method, money from a foreign country is lent to one or more banks in a developing country at a very low interest rate, and then the banks on-lend the money to individual enterprises. The aim is to support the small- and medium-sized private firms that are vitally important for the future of that country, but which lack the collateral usually required by the commercial banks.

This system has been in operation in only a few countries. Typical examples include Japan's ODA to both Tunisia and Hungary. The JEXIM (Export-Import Bank of Japan) lent money to the Tunisian Development Bank in the form of two-step loans, and the Tunisian Development Bank on-lent the money to individual enterprises. When the Japanese went to the bank to appraise the impact of their loan, they found that of the $170 million loans given to the bank, up to one hundred projects were carried out and about 10,000 jobs were created in Tunisia as a direct result. Similarly, in Hungary a loan was made in 1992 and approximately $130 million was given to ten banks.

In both Tunisia and Hungary, the Japanese loans not only helped to create jobs and increase economic activities, but they also filled the vacuum in two countries that did not have strong capital markets. They also helped the SMIs, especially where the commercial bank lending rate was between 30% and 45% interest, which is very common in developing countries. Such levels of interest no doubt discourage the business community from taking investment risks.

Other Forms of Raising Capital

There are other forms of raising capital such as stock exchanges, business angels, venture capital and private equity. These are mainly facilities by which private and public companies raise expansion capital. This book explores how the government can make use of the first two forms.

Stock Exchanges

Stock exchanges originated as mutual organizations. This means they existed for the members to benefit from the services they provided and were owned by their members (but not by having shares). Later, stock exchanges were demutualized, whereby the members sold their shares by issuing common stocks or shares to the public. In this way, the mutual organization became a corporation with shares listed on a stock exchange. The first company to issue stocks and bonds was the Dutch East India Company in 1602. In 1688 the trading of stocks began in the London Stock Exchange.

Although stock exchanges or capital markets mainly provide facilities for raising capital for business expansion, the government at various levels may decide to borrow money in order to finance infrastructural projects, such as rural electrification, sewage, water treatment or housing estates, by selling bonds to the public. In addition, to make regular payments on these bonds, the government refunds the principal when the bonds mature. Most developing countries have stock exchanges, and in these countries they can be characterized as quasi-state institutions.

Business Angels/Dragons' Den

Business angels are rich individuals who invest capital in small businesses and in return ask for equity shares in the business. Most of them are successful business people who would like to help the young entrepreneurs to grow. They not only provide the money but also useful advice and contacts to the businesses in which they invest. Some might work for the company on a part-time or full-time basis, but others might only attend the board meetings.

However, the problem is how to find such business angels. A state or local government that owns a television channel may find business angels by sponsoring, say, a TV programme that could bring out patriotic rich individuals who would like to invest in viable businesses and talented individuals within their areas. A typical example of such a television programme is Dragons' Den. This is an adventure-capitalist television programme that originated in Japan, where the format is owned by Sony. The "dragons" are five rich entrepreneurs who invest their money in potentially viable business proposals. People or existing business people who have good business ideas but lack money and direction make their presentations to the "dragons" in the hope of encouraging them to become investors. Once the contestant has made his or her presentation, the "dragons" will then probe the ideas further. Then, either individually or jointly, they may make an offer of cash and will ask for a certain percentage of the business equity in return. Other "dragons" may see the idea as unprofitable and as such will reject the investment opportunity.

Apart from Japan, Dragons' Den has been launched in a number of countries. In the UK, it is broadcast by the BBC and hosted by a former BBC economics editor, Evan Davis. Developing countries may wish to emulate such programmes and this could trigger business activities, leading to the creation of jobs in those countries.

CHAPTER FIVE
Technology Transfer Mechanisms

Definitions

Technology here refers to the knowledge and procedures used to transform inputs derived from the natural environment into useful outputs, normally called goods and services. It goes from conceptualization to creation. An appropriate definition of technology, provided by the World Intellectual Property Organization (WIPO), is as follows:

Technology means systematic knowledge for the manufacture of a product, the application of a process or the rendering of a service, whether that knowledge be reflected in an invention, an industrial design, a utility, a model, or a new plant variety, or in technical information or skills, or in the services or assistance provided by experts for the design and installation, operation or maintenance of an industrial plant or for the management of an industrial or commercial enterprise or its activities.

International technology transfer is a complex process, which not only brings two independent states into contact, but also brings two or more enterprises into mutual cooperation. As we can see from the above definition, technology involves the flow of information, the granting of industrial property rights, and the construction of a factory, accompanied by a transfer of technical knowledge from one country to another. It distinguishes itself from domestic transfers, which may go from one city to another. In precise terms, transfer of technology entails all the transactions and procedures required to get a plant into industrial production, such as:

- The granting of industrial property rights;
- The provision of services in the training of staff;
- The installation of managerial, marketing and distribution procedures;
- Sale or lease of machinery along with technical knowhow;
- The commissioning of an industrial plant.

Technology flows across national boundaries in many different ways. Methods used can be classified into two different groups – informal and formal. The informal groups include trade fairs, students, publications, seminars and migration of skilled personnel. The formal methods of technology transfer range from "packaged" technology (where the supplier's sale is a one-off transaction, and they have no more business with the buyer regarding the technology) to complex technology transfer transactions involving one or more of the above-mentioned procedures.

The United Nations Centre on Transnational Corporations defined the formal methods of transfer of technology as falling into the following categories: Foreign Direct Investment with foreign control; joint ventures where the foreign technology seller holds a minority equity; licensing; franchising; management contracts; marketing and technical services contracts; and international sub-contracting. Although there are merits and shortcomings attached to each of these methods, the success and configuration of the technology depends on the nature of the technology concerned, the strategy and capabilities of the buyer, the strategy of the seller and particularly, the policies of the supplier and buyer governments. For Western governments, technology is a "public good" – not totally in the hands of individual investors or multinational corporations. The government will not leave the dissemination of technological information entirely to the market mechanism. It will decide which has to be disseminated to other nations, and also which technology must not be exported for security or other reasons. Such control covers both government-sponsored R&D as well as R&D sponsored by private corporations. In fact, there is no doubt about the dominant position of Western governments. Without their support, industrialization may not begin in most developing countries. They are the homes of the giant MNCs, whose policies determine how much industrialization can take place in the developing countries through their control of finance and technology.

Foreign Direct Investment (FDI)

Foreign direct investment is a full combination of capital, technology, management and commercial expertise. It is a "packaged" technology, implanted in another country. In accepting this kind of investment, the host country acquires some technology ipso facto. Technological knowhow is diffused because the multinationals will be using local sub-contractors. It will train local manpower both at operational and supervisory levels. The multinationals prefer direct international investment to any other form of technology transfer because they are unwilling to share their decision-making powers or competitive advantages with anyone.

However, FDI is more controversial than other channels of technology transfer. This is because views on its desirability range from those of the "dependency" theorists, who regard it as a continuing source of underdevelopment, to those who regard it as the only practical source of employment opportunities for the large numbers of unemployed people in less developed countries. The scholars of the dependency theory believe that the world trading system tends to keep most developing states in a condition of economic and political bondage, resulting in a neo-imperial and neo-colonial relationship between the rich and poor countries. For many supporters of this theory, these conditions must be destroyed and replaced with a new international economic order that could end the dependency of Third World states. They argue that Western MNCs effectively control the economies of many developing countries through their global and local economic powers in order to exploit and take excessive profits back to the West, instead of providing welfare for those in the host states. They suggest that there can be no repeat of the experiences of the advanced Western states because it is argued that they industrialized at the expense of the less developed countries.

On the other hand, there are other theorists who suggest that the relations of the underdeveloped states with the developed world are not on an equal basis, and that the only recourse for states in Africa and Asia is self-reliance, or cooperation with other states in a similar situation. This group advocates economic nationalism and serious planning for growth so as to avoid the distortions of the global market and the multinational corporations.

The question is, how can the technological gap between the haves and the have-nots be bridged when the United Nations agencies' emphasis on solutions that might help develop Third World countries has not always been shared by the industrialized states? The GATT has ceased to exist. The WTO will also go without success from the point of view of developing nations. As for economic nationalism, the word "nationalism" has not been a common term but its application in every aspect of our daily life is an open secret. Economic nationalism was predicted by critics of FDI, who also claimed that the advantages of FDI were exaggerated. They argued that many multinationals limit the transfer of skills by using expatriate staff in all the important positions. They also claimed that foreign firms hinder the development of local firms, as many of them invest simply to exploit cheap labour and natural resources without making proper and equitable payments.

Whatever reasons are put forward against FDI, it is more attractive than foreign borrowing, as it involves the transfer of technical and managerial skills from developed countries, and provides capital and industrial technology. In particular, it has access to overseas markets and does not impose a burden of debt on the government. It might, therefore, be viewed as an almost ideal way of providing employment opportunities for the under-employed labour force. Other benefits include the stimulation of local economic activities, which inevitably lead to increases in national income. In short, FDI should be seen as a complement to local entrepreneurial efforts, as long as the developing nations apply some level of a local content requirement (as illustrated in Chapter Three) and put some reasonable conditions in place. But it may also require market liberalization and the offering of incentives to the FDI provider. Liberalization and incentives in themselves are not enough to improve the prospects for attracting them. Economic and political conditions, availability of skilled labour, efficient supply and distribution networks, efficient infrastructure, good prospects for demand growth and suitable social conditions within potential host countries could all influence where the FDI chooses to locate.

Another important feature hitherto unknown to many developing countries' industrial planners is the Investment Guarantee Schemes, which some of the developed countries administer. These schemes cover certain economic and political risks that are associated with investment in developing countries. The investment guarantee schemes of individual developed countries vary widely in their coverage, but Table 8 (shown later in this chapter) outlines the guarantee schemes offered by most developed countries. The multinational organizations take into consideration their own government's cover in a particular developing country before they consider whether or not to invest in that country. Political leaders from developing countries have to lobby the Western countries in order to have their countries included in their Investment Guarantee Schemes. That opens the way for foreign investors!

The Joint Venture (JV) as a Transfer Mode

Joint ventures may be defined as collaborations on investments involving shared ownership between local and foreign partners. The parties to a joint venture may be individuals, corporate bodies, governments or governmental agencies, and the agreement may be bipartite or multipartite. There are two fundamental forms of joint venture: contractual and equity.

Contractual joint ventures are normally used for the supply of capital, equipment, industrial property, technical assistance and knowhow by the foreign partners to the local partner in return for royalties, which are calculated on the basis of production, sales, and profits and so on. Other contractual joint ventures involve only licensing and knowhow or marketing arrangements.

Equity joint ventures are by far the most common form of joint venture involving foreign investment. They imply the participation of two or more partners in the equity capital of a local company. The equity share may be in the form of minority foreign ownership, majority foreign ownership or shared ownership. Control depends on the form of input variables contributed by the partners concerned.

The joint venture, as a channel for the transfer of technology, constitutes one of the most important instruments of economic cooperation. It can be seen as a marriage between two foreign firms or nations and, as in all marriages, the success of the undertaking depends on mutual accommodation. A joint venture involves, to varying degrees, the sharing of equity capital control, profit or loss and decision-making authority. Like FDI, it brings in foreign capital, technology and knowhow. The Joint Venture has been used successfully by many of the newly industrializing economies (NIEs) to enhance their economic development, improve their competitiveness in international markets, and as a learning device that interacts with domestic technological efforts. All these can be achieved by developing nations should they choose a joint venture option. In short, in a country like the Republic of Korea, there are very few wholly owned foreign subsidiaries, and most of the transnational corporations there are in the form of joint ventures. This has helped to promote economic cooperation between the Republic of Korea and foreign countries, and also strengthens their international competitiveness as well as inducing the development of necessary advanced technology. China, in her quest for industrialization, has also adopted a joint venture approach since 1979. The Sino-foreign joint ventures law provides for three forms of transfer of technology through joint ventures: licensing from the foreign partners, licensing from a third party and equity capitalization of the intellectual property rights or technical knowhow of foreign partners. Under the jointly owned company's category, the firms in most developing countries are the junior partners. But they gain direct access to training and advanced technology while the foreign firm secures low-cost production. The success of the developing countries in achieving their objectives depends on their resources, development level and absorptive capabilities.

Let us look at the three methods generally used by Sino-foreign joint ventures engaging in the transfer of technology:

- Licensing – the partners of joint ventures can grant the joint venture the right to use the technology by signing a separate licensing contract with it. The licensing contract must be one of the appendices to the joint venture contract.

- Imports from a third party – the joint venture may import technology from a third party. The third party is required to sign a technology import contract with the joint venture.

- Value Appraisal – the foreign investor in a joint venture may contribute an industrial property right or technical knowhow as an investment, the value of which can be assessed. The dividends may be divided in proportion to the shares of equity held. The following conditions must, however, be observed:

    o The foreign investor must ensure that it is the rightful owner of the technology provided;

    o The foreign investor must be capable of manufacturing new products urgently needed in China, or products suitable for export;

    o The evaluation of the price of all introduced technology by reference to international practice has to be ascertained through consultation among the parties to the joint venture on a fair and reasonable basis, or evaluated by terms agreed upon by the parties to the joint venture;

    o The foreign investors must present the requisite documents relating to the industrial property rights or knowhow, including photocopies of the patents, certificates or trademark registration certificates, and particulars of the state of validity, technical characteristics, price and the price agreement signals with the Chinese partners. All the documents must be appended to the joint venture contract.

In the Republic of Korea, the guidelines for all foreign investments, including joint ventures, include:

- Minimum foreign investment;
- Approval of eligible projects;
- Foreign investment procedures.

In Ghana, the criteria for approval of technology transfer agreements include the following:

- Technology should be relevant and appropriate to the conditions and needs of Ghana.
- The production process should, as far as practicable, utilize Ghana's raw materials, supplies, personnel and services.
- As far as practicable, the production process should be labour-intensive.
- The technology must be proven and evidence should be provided to show that the process has been utilized in other countries with conditions and needs similar to those of Ghana.
- Payment for the technology should be fair and reasonable, having regard, inter alia, to the nature of the technology, its value to the national economy and the technology's recipients, and the duration of the technology transfer agreement.

The Ghana criteria also added that the following "Restrictive Practices" are, as a rule, prohibited in technology agreements:

- "Tied" purchases from the technology's suppliers or a party nominated by them.
- Export restrictions (i.e. pertaining to territories/countries where the recipient should not export the patented goods).
- Pricing of products (i.e. restrictions in the determination of prices, component prices or discounts for products made under licence).
- Undue interference in the management and control of the recipient company.
- Restrictions on acquiring technology from any other source.
- Free "grant-back clauses" (i.e. the recipient is requested to grant back to the supplier an assignment or an exclusive licence with regard to any improvement that the recipient makes within the scope of the licensed technology).

- Litigation regarding patent infringements (i.e. the technology supplier shall be responsible for taking legal action on any patent infringements in the recipient's country).

These conditions are similar to many other countries' criteria. They do not stop the foreign investors from coming into the country. As much as the developing countries want FDIs and joint ventures, and promise them some incentives and protections, they do not have to give them a blank cheque. Instead, what the foreign investors value much more is the protection of their intellectual property rights, which is further discussed below. Simply put, the investors are more concerned with the spill over effects of the technological knowhow.

FDI is a bit controversial, especially because unlike joint ventures, the investors have total control over how to transfer their technology and run their business. Their normal practice even includes entering into specific contracts with employees in order to protect all the knowhow and innovations developed in their firm, while entering into a joint venture means the extension of knowhow to the local partner, who may someday become a major partner.

The host country must establish some levels of protection for the interests of its native enterprises as well as for the interests of the owners of the intangible property. The legislation must, however, balance between the objective of attracting foreign investors and the goal of protecting native enterprises. The existence of the understated conflicting interests (see Table 6) can affect access to technology in joint ventures.

Table 6: Conflict of Interest in Joint Venture Agreements

Interests of TNC	Interests of Recipient
Sales in local market	Export possibilities
Transfer of profits	Retention of profits
Control of joint venture	Joint control
Supply of spares	Free to place orders

Less equity	More equity
More intangibles	More tangibles: cash
Local loans	Foreign financing
R&D abroad	R&D at home
Protection of foreign property	Against abuse of patent
Savings in labour	Pay at local standards
Limiting of export/territories	No restrictions
Limiting of choice of technology	No restrictions
No right to improvements	Right to improvements
Limitation of guarantee	Full guarantee

However, these many conflicts of interest between the joint partners are not the only obstacles in the transfer of technology. For example, the exporting venture partners must also be sensitive to anti-trust laws in their countries of operation. Both the US anti-trust laws and the EU Treaty of Rome laws extend to joint venture in foreign countries, if:

- One of the participants is a citizen of the United States or of an EU country, respectively; or
- If the use of the technology outside the home country adversely and significantly affects the import and export of goods in the home country.

The laws apply to any joint venture whose activities abroad affect their nations' competitiveness in a given market. Then, how can one reconcile such anti-trust laws with the international instruments on liberalization of trade?

Licensing as a Transfer Method

Under the pressure of import penetration, the need to advance technological capabilities and competitiveness, domestically owned firms are usually impelled to license from overseas enterprises. Such licences also help them to diversify their firm's production. The technological agreements of firms cover a wide range of issues from "knowhow" for the implementation of productive processes, the granting of rights for patent exploitation and the use of brand names, to technical consulting. These are sources of competitive advantage, which is the main reason for obtaining overseas licenses and leads owners to increase the margins of their pricing policies. Consequently, such increases lead to higher profits for the licensing firm. Licensing agreements may also affect the export performance of the firm receiving the license. It may result in the possibility of the licensing firm increasing its turnover by undertaking export activities within the boundaries stipulated in the agreement. Therefore, the firm uses a licensing agreement not only to capture the local market but also as an instrument for increasing global profits. On the other hand, the firm makes royalty payments to the licensor.

There are three major forms of licensing: patents, trademarks and franchises, which can be illustrated using simulated examples, as follows:

(Although distributorship may be regarded as a form of licensing, since they do not require technology transfer they will not be discussed here.)

Patents:

Inventor Y in a developed country owns valuable patents for the manufacture of drugs for the treatment of malaria. Rather than manufacturing the drug itself, Inventor Y hopes to license its rights under the patent to drug companies in various countries. Inventor Y has already registered a patent with each country's national registrar. One such drug manufacturing company is located in a country in Africa. That drug manufacturer is duly licensed under local law, obtains all the correct permits from local authorities and purchases from Inventor Y, by means of a patent license, the right to use Inventor Y's information, which had been protected by the patent. To protect itself from local or other foreign competitors, the drug company files an application for a patent for the drug under local law. Under FDI, JV or trademarks, the investor's reputation and goodwill are not linked to the drug manufacturer in Africa. Consequently, the limits on the licensee's discretion in conducting its own operation are less burdensome, but the amount of compensation to Inventor Y may be high.

Trademark:

Company A, after discovering a potential market opportunity in a country in Asia for its products, licenses a local manufacturer called Company B to manufacture the product and affix A's trademark to it. Company B is then permitted, through the licensing agreement, to sell the goods in the specified territory, its own country and a bordering country in Asia. The value of the trademark license lies mainly in the right to use Company A's trademark, and the license requires that the local manufacturer fulfils certain quality requirements set out by Company A. As long as Company B maintains the standards and pays the required royalty, Company B may use its own manufacturing knowhow.

Franchise:

Company X owns a chain of restaurants and wishes to set up a new one in a South American country. Due to its reputation for high quality food and customer service, Company X wishes to have a business arrangement that will protect its image. It enters into a franchise agreement with Company Y in South America, which means that Company Y cannot operate the restaurant in any manner they like without Company X's consent or approval. Company Y knows that Company X has a reputation and their trademark and license will attract a lot of customers. Company Y is prepared to take any instructions from Company X, including regular training and seminars for all their franchise managers. Following the Quality Assurance Guide, Company Y must employ managers approved by Company X. Company Y must receive a supply of accessories such as plates, towels and equipment from Company X. The franchise agreement is therefore a trademark with special requirements for quality control. The franchisee pays a royalty to the franchisor.

Abuses and Compulsory Licensing

In addition to the anti-trust laws existing in some developed countries, the licensors of patents from developed countries have often abused the patent rights. A typical example might occur where a patent holder who has no immediate intention of licensing his invention overseas files for protection abroad and then refuses to work the patent. The reason for this refusal is mainly to control the market in a country by preventing the manufacture and importation into it of any goods but those of the patent holder. This means that no one can compete with him because his patent exists in that developing country. But in actual fact, the developing country has not received such technological knowledge – it can only import the patent holder's product. In response to abuses of this nature, many developing countries' governments now declare the original patent invalid, and in turn require compulsory licensing or licenses of right to be issued to new applicants. An applicant for a compulsory license must justify this license in the particular circumstances of the case. This is because it is an authorization, to an entity or person other than the original patent holder, to proceed without such a patent holder's consent – enabling actions which would otherwise be prohibited by the patent holder. Other abuses of licensing agreements by transnational corporations in their dealings with less sophisticated entities in developing countries result mainly from the latter's unequal bargaining power. For a typical example, see Case Study 9 in Chapter Six.

Turnkey Transfer Operations

In a turnkey transfer operation the supplier is responsible for the whole technology from the basic design to the "turning of the key" by the purchaser. The responsibility itself covers not only the functioning of the separate parts of the project, but also the proper functioning of the whole plant within a fixed time limit. Whether the payment for the technology is to be made by a lump sum or by installments, the control and ownership passes to the purchaser as soon as he is handed the key. The package comes with the training of operatives and guarantees. It might be more expensive than buying separate units from different countries and putting them together under a project manager. This latter process is called unbundling (see below), but the risk is that the recipient of technology will not have any operational guarantee for the whole industry.

Unbundling

Due to the problems associated with FDI, JV and licensing, other advanced developing countries have tried to promote a policy of unbundling. The principle underlying the unbundling policy is the separation of the foreign technology from the ownership and management. The host country or the purchaser acquires full ownership of the foreign technology. The unbundling policy may give rise to the following measures:

1) Make pre-investment studies, appoint project managers and train up the local workforce.

2) Buy separately the constituent components of the successive stages in the process and recombine them with a project manager who coordinates all the activities. In this way, they may obtain a more advantageous price than by buying a turnkey unit, and this also has the option of subcontracting certain peripheral items to local firms. Unlike turnkey operation, there is no performance guarantee on this project.

3) Finance the technology purchase through cumulative savings or through borrowing abroad to finance part of it. Borrowing abroad may be better where the local interest rate is too high. It must be paid back out of earnings from the project concerned. Alternatively, the project may be privatized (sold) as soon as it is completed.

The developing country or the purchaser takes control of the production operation. This means that if there are enough local skills, the imported technology can be exploited. Admittedly, some of the least developed countries have tried to transfer technology through the unbundled channel without success. They end up incurring more debts. This is because most of them choose the most expensive projects, such as heavy steel industries, heavy chemical industries or heavy petrochemical industries. But some more advanced developing countries have benefited from the unbundling policy by choosing light industries where they enjoyed comparative advantages such as footwear, textiles, chipboard, cement, and particular-

ly food industries. In this way, the development of small- medium-sized industries would benefit the developing countries via:
- Employment
- Capital saving
- Mastery of technology
- Satisfaction of basic needs.

Intellectual Property Rights

For the private inventor and MNC alike, technology is like any other product. It has its economic rent. The economic rent is the incentive to produce and to make profits. This is the dilemma partly faced by the intellectual property rights such as patents, copyrights and trademarks, which give the owner a monopoly to sell his technology for a limited period. The basic rationale for intellectual property protection has been to encourage inventors and to promote national technological and industrial development. For this reason, the leading industrialized countries have made intellectual property rights protection a basis on which to liberalize trade and to encourage foreign direct investment and technology flow.

The standards for intellectual property protection proposed by the leading industrialized countries are as follows:
1. The patentability of all inventions, regardless of subject matter. Such protection must confer exclusive use and manufacturing and commercial rights for at least 20 years.
2. Protection of trademarks, including service marks, well-known marks and geographical names, on the basis of use or registration, for no less than ten-year terms with an indefinite number of renewals, and excluding others from using the same or similar marks for the same or similar goods.
3. Copyright protection for all forms of original expression, regardless of the medium, and comprising exclusive commercial, distribution and reproduction rights for the life of the author plus 50 years.
4. Legal protection for any original layout design of semi-conductor chips or integrated circuits, in the form of exclusive use, reproduction and commercial rights for at least ten years.
5. Limitation of compulsory licensing to situations recognised in relevant international conventions or for reasons of national emergency or violation of anti-trust or competition laws, with such licensing to

be non-exclusive and subject to payment of compensation at market value.

6. Enforcement measures, including the imposition of civil and criminal penalties, to deter infringements of intellectual property rights and trade in infringing goods both internally and at national borders.

7. The application of national treatment, most-favoured nation treatment and transparency standards to intellectual property laws and regulations.

However, there are divided views on the extent to which intellectual property protection actually promotes technology transfer. Some people contend that countries with inadequate levels of intellectual property protection would be unable to attract high levels of trade, investment and technology flow, as the owners of intellectual property would be unwilling to enter into such transactions without the requisite protection. The developing countries have argued that the levels of intellectual property protection and the conditions attached to such protection should be left largely to the discretion of each country, as is currently the case under a number of international instruments. There are over eighty international instruments and numerous sub-regional and bilateral agreements that contain measures related to the transfer of technology and intellectual property rights. The intellectual property provisions contained in such instruments depend on the objectives and purposes of the technology transfer in terms of nature and methods. But the adoption of such instruments is an expression of states' willingness to cooperate internationally in order to redress the distribution of technological capabilities in the world. Each of the instruments contains both legally binding and non-binding stipulations. However, according to the 2001 UNCTAD Compendium on Transfer of Technology Instruments, all the various instruments aim to promote access to Western technologies in the developing countries, particularly in the least developed countries. These instruments are too numerous to be listed here. Apart from the international treaties or instruments, the future of developing countries' economic growth depends not only on their vast natural resources but also on the nation's ability to harness the innovation potential in their people. Intellectual property rights are a key component of any innovation system, because they grant an innovator compensation for the investment of time and resources that went into the creation of a new product or technology.

Major Issues and Arguments

Views and wishes of the different actors, as presented by Howard Perlmutter and Tagi Sagafi-Nejad, can be seen in Table 7.

Table 7: TOT: Major Issues and Arguments

Issues and Actors	Supplier Firms (TNCs)	Recipient Government (LICS)	Recipient Firms Technology (LICS)	Supplier Government
Contribution	We do the best we can under each circumstance but local government and firms are also responsible for maximizing the contribution of imported technology.	Imported technology must be appropriate. It must contribute to any technological growth, and dependence. Most technologies are inappropriate	Technology we receive must strengthen us and make us self-sufficient. Sometimes we do not receive the support we expect from suppliers.	Impact of imported technology depends on host government's policy and available capacity as well as on TNCs. TNCs alone should not be blamed for poor impact.
Control of technology	We must control our technology and how it is utilized, so we can maintain our competitive position and improve upon our technology. It is our most important	We have control over imported technology, to improve our science and technology position. Lack of local control hinders our policies.	We do not feel as though technology belongs to us, so we do not make every effort to improve it. If we had full control we would use technology	You cannot expect a private firm which has spent millions of dollars and resources on developing a technology to forfeit its right to control completely. Each recipient is but one of

	asset.		better or would improve it ourselves.	many. Suppliers need to maintain control.
Restrictive transfer practices	If we require safeguards or certain quality standards or have other requirements, it is only because we care about our quality, reputation and the preservation of our markets and competitive position.	Restrictive and abusive practices of TNCs have drained our treasuries while keeping us dependent and technologically backward.	Some restrictions make it costly or uneconomical for us to have contracts for acquisition of foreign technology but we need them to grow, make new and better products and sell more. Restrictions inhibit us.	Restrictive practices which impede the functioning of the market are prohibited by our laws, which are sufficient to prevent such practices. But most of what recipients call restrictive practices are the normal outcome of bargaining situations.
Price	We have spent much time and money and sell our technology in the market like any other item. If we do not get the right price, we will not transfer our technology.	Technology suppliers must charge us the marginal cost of technology, as our markets were not the prime motive for the initial development of their technologies.	Price of technology often too high for us to afford but we have to pay what they ask for.	Price is always subject to the laws of supply and demand. Buyers and sellers are mature and can agree without government interference.

Government control (income tax, patents)	Too much government control hampers our operations, reduces our effectiveness.	We must have control over our society and the use of our productive resources.	We need freedom from unnecessary government interference, but we also need government protection.	Unless matters of national interest are involved, firms must remain as free as possible.
Protection of proprietary rights	We need confidentiality and protection for our most important assets. Without it, there would be no incentive to develop new technology and to transfer it.	We need the information for strengthening our national techno-logical capacity. TNCs are too restrictive and secretive about their technology.	We respect the desire of suppliers for confidentiality and abide by our contracts. But if a needed technology is too costly or unobtainable from the source, we will copy it if we can.	One cannot expect owners of technology to give away their major assets.

Source: Perlmutter and Sagafi-Nejad, 1981: 26–27

The objectives of these actors differ greatly and from the above table one can see the whole range of constraints and complexities in the international transfer of technology process. There are two outstanding points to observe, i.e. the major problems encountered and the profit/business motive. As for the latter motive, why should the owner of technology want to pass it on in the first place? The prerequisite of any successful passing on must be self-interest, and that self-interest is guided by profit. In addition to the views expressed by the four actors above, let us look at some other points worth remembering in some of the issues.

Contribution of the Technology

The impact of imported technology depends largely on three factors:

1. The supplier firm's willingness to support the plants, e.g. releasing necessary documents, technical support, training of staff, and price of technology and services rendered.
2. The recipient firm's capability to absorb the new technology, ability to modify, negotiating skills, available finance, etc.
3. The recipient government's assistance in fashioning policies that are conducive to the business climate, the availability of essential infrastructure, assistance in transferring technology, and insisting on and monitoring the local content requirement. For example, to maximise the contribution of direct foreign investment, a local content requirement should be embodied in the agreement between the suppliers of technology and the recipient country. However, the local content requirement must be in areas of local capabilities, such as skilled labour and abundant raw materials. As we saw in Chapter Three, in the European Union the local content requirement is 80%, below which the output of such establishments is regarded as non-European in origin, and as such may be liable to import duties.

In the case of developing countries, the degree or percentage may vary according to the level of particular raw materials, components and availability of skilled labour. A typical example of local content/input for the automobile industry consists of tyres, batteries, paints, upholstery, labour and so on. Meanwhile, the major problem of the local content issue may not only be how to formulate the policies but also that of monitoring the formulated policies, as well as developing basic industries to provide the required local material inputs to potential producers. If implemented, it will increase employment opportunities, not only in the imported technology factories but also, more essentially, in the raw material/component production sectors, thereby increasing the number of potential indigenous technological innovations. It is this process that one may call the developmental impact of technology or the multiplier effect of technology transfer.

Control of Technology

The four actors view the control of any technology transferred differently. Whether the control of technology should be in the hands of suppliers or recipients will depend on the nature of the contract they enter into. As for FDI, suppliers take the majority equity and in most cases 100% equity. They do this because they prefer not to share their decision-making power or competitive advantage with respect to costs, technology and product differentiation with any other suppliers. In the case of joint ventures, the control also depends on the level of equity participation between the foreign suppliers and local entrepreneurs, while in the case of licensing contracts, the technology is usually controlled by the licensee.

On the other hand, the host country's patent law allows the inventor of a technology to benefit and control his invention for a given period of time. Importantly, too, the host country makes laws and procedures governing infringement and remedies. The host country may also create a specific administrative body to regulate transfers of technology. The body can give its approval before any kind of technology is brought into the country, and may review the contract agreement between the supplier and the recipient organizations.

Price of Technology

Technology is like any other product. There may be cartels in one developed country or region, but it is not easy to have a worldwide cartel in industrial technology. Even in military technology such as nuclear weapons it has not been easy to stop proliferation. International institutions such as the Missile Technology Control Regime (MTCR) have found it difficult to stop the proliferation of missile technology in developing countries. Therefore, it is safe to assume that an industrial civil technology without any international regulatory body hindering its transfer can be accessed worldwide. All the developing countries need is the ability to "shop around" and compare quality as well as price (including transportation costs) of the technology they want to acquire.

Restrictive Transfer Practices

Restrictions on the transfer of technology in international commerce predate the days of ancient Rome, during which considerable efforts were expended in keeping the mixture of sulphur, pitch and charcoal known as "Greek fire" a secret. Sithoff states that legal restrictions on technology transfer have been based on restricting the exportation of technology to a country only when such technology could be damaging to the originating country when in the hands of a potential aggressor. On the other hand, legislators, in making laws to protect the export of "big fish" technologies, have fashioned a net so fine that it typically strains even the sardines from the sea. Western restrictions should not include all technologies that are subject to patent applications and, according to Peter Montagnon (1990), rich industrialized nations are using strategic export restrictions as a cover to monopolize the commercial exploitation of new technologies. There cannot be any realistic effort to transfer industrial technology to the developing world if restrictions are allowed to continue. In fact, in applying the transfer of technology code, the International Court of Justice should take into account unfair restrictive clauses which the technology suppliers place on the developing countries. A list of these can be seen in Chapter Six under Restrictive Business Practices.

Foreign Investment Guarantee Schemes

In addition to the intentions expressed by the developed countries in various instruments, i.e. promising access to Western technologies for developing countries, a number of developed countries, international agencies and multinational organizations have "Investment Guarantee Schemes" in place. These schemes are supposed to be for the developing countries' benefit, and constitute a kind of insurance cover for the international companies wishing to invest in some developing countries. It covers against risks like expropriation, exchange transfer blockage, war damage, insurrection, commercial risk and political risk. The covers help to attract FDI into the developing countries that can benefit from it. These opportunities are there for the government and enterprises of the developing countries to harness, but what this book has not uncovered is whether there are concessions to be made before such guarantee cover is given to any country.

Table 8 gives examples of Investment Guarantee Schemes.

Table 8: Foreign Investment Guarantee Schemes

Country/ multilateral agency	Administration	Type of risk covered	Criteria for coverage
Australia	Export Finance and Insurance Corporation	Expropriation, exchange transfer blockage, war damage	-
Austria	Osterreichische Kontrollbank	Three main political risks	Applies to both developed and developing countries
Belgium	Office National du Ducroire	Political risk	Project must contribute to the economic and social development of recipient country; it must promote Belgium's economic interests abroad
Canada	Export Development Corporation	Transfer of funds, expropriation, war, revolution or insurrection	Scheme available only to new investments
Denmark	Danish International Development Agency	Three main political risks	New investments only, where investor has control over enterprise. Investment must have positive developmental effect on host country's economy
Finland	Export Guarantee Board	Expropriation, serious disturbance in economic condition of host country, restrictions in capital and earnings	Investment must be in form of equity participation, loans or loan guarantees or licensees
Federal	Inter-ministerial	Expropriation,	New____ investments only,

Republic of Germany	Committee from Ministries of Economy, Finance, Foreign Affairs and Economic Cooperation	nationalization, war revolution, non-transferability of capital and earnings	positive effect on home and host country economy. Situation in host country must appear satisfactory at time of approval with respect to legal protection against political risks. Existence of bilateral investment treaty is a pre-condition
Japan	Ministry of International Trade and Industry	War, expropriation, exchange transfer and commercial risk (bankruptcy)	Direct investment by Japanese or non-Japanese company, portfolio investment and long-term loans for Japanese and non-Japanese companies if engaged in exploitation of mineral and natural resources
Netherlands	Netherlands Credit Insurance Company	Expropriation, nationalization, war, revolution, non-transferability of capital and earnings	New investments in developing countries, subject to satisfactory procedural arrangements for dealing with disputes
New Zealand	Export Guarantee Office	Exchange transfer expropriation, war damage	New equity investments
Sweden	Swedish Export Credits Guarantee Board	Currency transfer, expropriation and war	Investment must have positive impact on Swedish economy
Switzerland	Department of Economic Affairs	Three main types of political risk	Equity participation, only few investments promoting economic development of host country and reinvested earnings
United	Export Credits	Expropriation, war, restriction of	New investments, assisting in the development of host

Kingdom	Guarantee	remittances	country
United States	Overseas Private Investment Corporation	Currency inconvertibility, expropriation, political violence	-
World Bank	Multilateral Investment Corporation	Issue of guarantees including insurance with, and reinsurance of, existing political risk insurers. In addition, risks covered include creeping expropriation, currency inconvertibility	Projects of clear development interest for host country

International Finance Corporation/ Guaranteed Recovery of Investment Principal	International Finance Corporation	Threat of capital loss	Benefits host country economy, project must show financial promise

Source: OECD, 1988

Foreign Consultants, Technocrats and Industrial Master Plans

The industrialization process has a diversity of models, because each country has its own unique characteristics reflecting the natural endowment, social virtues and externalities. But the series of lessons in this book can only be useful to those who actually appreciate what the book is talking about. Therefore, first and foremost is the formation of a cadre of technocrats. Their first duty is to design an industrial master plan, which will identify the country's major industry sectors that will spearhead the nation's industrialization programme. Their second duty is to promote opportunities for the maximum and efficient utilization of the country's abundant natural resources. They can be called any name, but in Taiwan they were called the Task Force. However, before illustrating a typical local task force, let us look at how Taiwan used foreign consultants. Having foreign advisers was very important in their National Science and Technology Programme – they were responsible for overseeing the implementation of the programme.

Case Study 5: Taiwan's Foreign Consultants

Policy is not formed entirely within the government. Taiwan has a large establishment of universities, research institutes, and consulting firms heavily involved in policy formulation, and foreign consultants have also been much used. Until the end of U.S. Aid in 1965, hundreds of U.S. Consultants were involved in industrial planning and project design work. The U.S. Mission had a staff of some 350 people, including consultants and contractors. Much of the industrial screening work was done by the J. G. White Engineering Corporation of New York, which kept an office in Taipei with twenty-five to thirty-five American staff members during the 1950s. Although U.S. Consultants were important during the 1950s and 1960s, they did not necessarily make the decisions. A senior U.S. Official in Taiwan in the early 1960s recalls how impressed he was by the ability of Taiwan officials to listen respectfully to all consultants, treat them all with hospitality, give them all the impression that their advice was invaluable – and then be very selective in deciding which advice to accept and which to reject. Indeed, there is said to have been a chronic state of tension between K. Y. Yin and the U.S. Mission in the final years of his life (Wade, 1990: 221).

The consultants made specific recommendations about which products should be encouraged in each of the industries they examined. These included electrical machinery, electronics, petrochemicals and machinery. Private consulting firms also advised on ways of funding the industries, such as the use of venture capital firms, foreign investment in the stock exchange via unit trusts, or offshore banking units. Raising funds through the stock exchange is fine except that only the big (listed) companies may get funding.

As for venture capitalists, they are averse to foreign investment and prefer growth or expanding business; otherwise some of them do bring their expertise and skills into the business and take equity as well. Personally, I feel that these funding suggestions are no better than Malaysia's sources of capital that we saw in the previous chapter. Attention should also be paid to how the Taiwanese officials treated the foreign consultants by giving them the impression that their advice was invaluable and then being very selective in deciding which advice to accept and reject. The developing countries should not simply accept all the dictates of foreign consultants.

Now let us look at the formation of a typical task force in Taiwan. The country identified the automation industry as a high priority and wanted to bring in local talent with requisite experience and dynamism.

Case Study 6: Taiwan's Task Force

The National Science and Technology programme placed particular emphasis on the need for Taiwan to introduce more automation into its industry. The question was how. One of the leading advocates of automation for Taiwan was Caspar Shih, a Taiwan-born engineer working for General Electric in Canada. He was concerned that by not moving away quickly enough from labour-intensive production processes, Taiwan risked being outcompeted either by highly automated production in the advanced countries or by countries with cheaper labour. On visits to Taiwan in the early 1980s, he lectured on the need for automation and proposed a task force to help firms automate. He was persuaded to take leave from his job in order to initiate the task force himself. He is now directly responsible to the Minister of Economic Affairs, and great importance is attached to his ready access to the minister. But officially, the task force is within the ambit of the Industrial Technology Research Institute, a parastatal organization, which means that its staff are recruited on conditions applicable to government scientists, considerably better than those of line civil servants. From a professional staff of five at the start of 1983, numbers grew to ninety by early 1984, and are expected to increase to near 150. All but two are engineers. It represents a major new concentration of engineering talent within the government, in a position to exercise influence across a wide range of sectors.

Its core work is to promote the introduction of automotive technology by individual firms. One method is by lectures: in 1983 some 9,000

---

business executives attended automation task force lectures. The more important method is the factory visit. Six hundred and fifty factories were visited in 1983, most more than once. The visiting teams found, however, that the first priority in most cases was not process automation but, in 35% of cases, simple "rationalization" of production, which involved rearrangements on the production line without adding capital or replacing labour. In other cases the visiting teams recommended computerisation of management information, packaging equipment improvements, and the likes. Where they recommend capital investment in a machine not made in Taiwan, they can use IDB's special innovation fund to cover the cost of importing it. And any applications for loans from the Strategic Industry Fund for the purposes of automation have to be approved by the task force (Wade, 1990: 21).

Case Study 7: Malaysia's Industrial Master Plan

The 1986–1995 Industrial Master Plan was aimed at refocusing the largely market-oriented economy to a target-oriented approach that emphasized greater investments in the manufacturing sector. The three objectives set out by the IMP are as follows:

1. To accelerate the growth of the manufacturing sector and to ensure a continued rapid expansion of the economy, as well as to provide a basis for meeting the social objectives consistent with the new economic policy.
2. To promote opportunities for the maximum and efficient utilization of the nation's abundantly endowed natural resources.
3. To build up the foundation for leapfrogging towards advanced industrial country status in the formation stage by increasing indigenous technological capability and competitiveness.

The IMP projected that the growth rate of the manufacturing sector was going to be 8.8% in real terms, so that by 1995 the share of manufacturing in GDP would rise to 23.9%. As a direct result, the manufacturing sector was expected to create substantial employment opportunities amounting to an additional 705,400 new jobs by 1995. To achieve all this and to spearhead the country to industrialization status, the IMP identified as priority the following ten major industry sectors:

Rubber Products

1. To encourage aggressive export promotion and the development of significant market niches of selected key rubber products, particularly tyres and latex-dipped goods, by improving the level of competitiveness through adopting cost-reduction measures and increasing productivity and product quality in order to meet the IMP's export targets.
2. To encourage greater foreign investment, especially by multinational corporations (MNCs), in order to gain access to export markets and attain greater cooperation with them on R&D activities.
3. To place Malaysia at the forefront of R&D in rubber product manufacturing as well as in natural rubber production through providing more financial support to local and overseas institutions.

Palm Oil Products

1. To rationalize the palm oil industry and fractionation sub-sectors in order to increase their efficiency and competitiveness in the export markets.
2. To promote oleochemicals as priority products and as leading export items.

Food Processing Industry

1. To extend the range of food products that could be import-substituted and to develop new product lines through effective R&D.
2. To seek ways and means of reducing production costs in the industry through innovative production processes.

Wood-Based Industry

1. To rationalize inefficient and uneconomical sawmills and plywood mills through diversification into the manufacturing of downstream products or to merge them into larger economic units.
2. To create a large production base through the establishment of furniture complexes and timber-processing zones.
3. To develop the technological base of the industry through the upgrading of design, product development, research into materials and production technology.

Chemical Industry
1. To stimulate the demand for fertilizers by optimizing their usage in the agricultural sector.
2. To maximise the utilization of palm oil-based industries in order to make Malaysia a significant exporter of soaps and detergents.
3. To identify and exploit chemical deposits which can be tapped for production of inorganic chemicals.
4. To create a pool of local technical expertise to enable proper transfer and adaptation of acquired technology.

Electronics and Electrical Industry
For the electronics industry:
1. To foster the development of supplier and support industries.
2. To encourage the production of higher value-added products and R&D activities, and to improve design capabilities within the sector.
3. To improve and upgrade the technology used in the existing semiconductor industry and to test activities in order to increase productivity.

For the electrical industry:
1. To enhance domestic technological capability through the encouragement of greater R&D activities, skill upgrading and product development within the sector in order to lessen the dependence on foreign designs for the manufacture of electrical products.
2. To foster the development of efficient ancillary industries to support the growth of the industry.

Transport Equipment Industry
1. To restructure and rationalize the existing motor vehicle assemblers in order to achieve economies of scale and to develop the national car project as the focal point for the manufacture of component parts.
2. To formulate an effective local content programme to ensure the industry's competitiveness.

Machinery and Engineering Industry

1. To upgrade the level of domestic technology in terms of both manufacturing and designing capabilities through the introduction of specific R&D training programmes.
2. To expand the local supply capability by providing greater encouragement and incentives for the sub-sectors to modernize and diversify into a wider range of components and services of acceptable standards and quality.
3. To specifically promote the production of certain core products such as moulds, tools and dyes, and castings and forgings, which are the components used extensively in the manufacture of most machinery and equipment, and to create demand for the establishment of a network of these primary supplies by inducing downstream users to buy their components from local producers.

Iron and Steel Industry

1. To rationalize and reorganize the industry, especially in the production of billets, bars, wire rods and light sections, which face problems of inefficiency, high cost of production, and considerable overcapacity.
2. To undertake programmes towards increasing efficiency, upgrading technology and reducing production cost, so as to enable the industry to be competitive in the export market.

Textile and Apparel Industry

1. To undertake a comprehensive rationalization and modernization programme through the improvement and upgrading of existing facilities with the support of adequate incentives, particularly in the textile sub-sectors of spinning, weaving and knitting.
2. To increase productivity and technology absorptive capacity, and enhancement of manpower training and technology transfer, in order to achieve international competitiveness (Ali, 1992: 49–51).

CHAPTER SIX
Legal Aspects of TOT to Developing Countries

The UNCTAD draft international code of conduct on the transfer of technology (TOT) to developing countries comprises a preamble and nine chapters covering the following:

- Definition and scope of application (chapter 1);
- Objectives and principles (chapter 2);
- National regulations of TOT transactions (chapter 3);
- Restrictive business practices (chapter 4);
- Responsibilities and obligations of parties to TOT transactions (chapter 5);
- Special treatment for developing countries (chapter 6);
- International collaboration (chapter 7);
- International institutional machinery (chapter 8);
- Applicable laws and settlement of disputes (chapter 9).

Let us look at the historical background to the code of conduct and some extracts from certain provisions in chapters 2, 4 and 6, as follows:

Historical Background

The 1964 report of the United Nations on "The role of Patents in the Transfer of Technology to Developing Countries" emphasized the need to explore possibilities for the adoption of legislation concerning the transfer of industrial technology. As a result, the Economic and Social Council of the United Nations requested the Secretary General of UNCTAD to examine the adequacy of existing national and international practices for the transfer of patented and unpatented technologies to developing countries. In turn, the UNCTAD Secretariat commissioned various studies on the transfer of technology to developing countries. Also, a unanimous intergovernmental resolution at the meeting of UNCTAD III held in Santiago, Chile in 1972 urged the developed countries to improve the means of access to technology, as well as the terms and conditions on which this technology could be obtained. It was also decided at the meeting that the Secretary General of UNCTAD should investigate the possibility of a new international regulation system for the transfer of patented and unpatented technologies to less developed countries.

The study was commissioned and prepared by a group of experts under the auspices of the Pugwash Conference on Science and World Affairs. Following their findings, a resolution of the intergovernmental group in July 1974 requested the Secretary General of UNCTAD to convene an intergovernmental group of experts to prepare a draft outline to serve as a basis for a universally applicable code of conduct. At the meetings of the Intergovernmental Group in 1975, proposals for a draft code were presented, first by Mexico on behalf of Group A (developing countries) and secondly, by Group B (Western industrialized countries).

The Group A proposal contained a number of issues on prohibited conduct, applicable to all contracts involving the transfer of technology including intra-enterprise transfers and joint venture agreements. The code was expressed as mandatory and contained chapters on special treatment for developing countries and on guarantees to be furnished by technology suppliers. But Group B's proposal was mainly on freedom-of-contract principles and said little about prohibited practices. Since then, a number of diplomatic rounds, including GATT and WTO, have not been able to resolve their differences over some of the issues in the TOT chapters. In short, it was because of the inability of GATT to reach a consensus that UN mandated the UNCTAD to examine the existing practices in the transfer of technology to developing countries.

Objectives and Principles

The four categories of objectives declared in the chapter on general objectives of the international code of conduct are as follows:

1) To establish general and equitable standards on which to base the relationship among parties to the transfer of technology transactions and governments concerned, taking into consideration their legitimate interests, and giving due recognition to the special needs of developing countries for the fulfilment of their economic and social development objectives.

2) To promote mutual confidence between parties as well as their governments.

3) To facilitate the formulation, adoption and implementation of national policies, laws and regulations on the subject of transfer of technology by setting forth international norms.

4) To set forth an appropriate set of responsibilities and obligations of parties to the transfer of technology transactions, taking into consideration their legitimate interests as well as differences in their bargaining position.

These are aimed at establishing the general norms for the transfer of technology – both within the developed world and to the developing countries. However, there are a number of other objectives specifically to facilitate the transfer of technology to developing countries. They are contained in paragraphs (iii), (v) and (vi) of the TOT code and state as follows:

(iii) To encourage transfer of technology transactions, particularly those involving developing countries, under conditions where bargaining positions of the parties to transactions are balanced in such a way as to avoid abuses of a stronger position and thereby mutual satisfactory agreements.

(v) To facilitate and increase the international flow of proprietary and non-proprietary technology for strengthening the growth of the scientific and technological capabilities of all countries, in particular, developing countries, so as to increase their participation in world production and trade.

(vi) To increase the contribution of technology towards the identification and solution of social and economic problems of all countries, particularly the developing countries, including the development of basic sectors of their national economies.

Also, the TOT covered some specific problems of developing countries by selecting appropriate technology and unpacking technology transactions. These are addressed in the objectives contained in paragraphs (iv) and (viii), as follows:

(iv) To facilitate and increase the international flow of technological information, particularly on the availability of alternative technologies as a prerequisite for the assessment, selection, adoption, development and use of technologies in all countries, particularly in developing countries.

(viii) To promote adequate arrangements as regards unpacking in terms of information concerning the various elements of the technology to be transferred, such as that required for technical, institutional and financial evaluation of the transaction, thus avoiding undue or unnecessary packaging.

Restrictive Business Practices

It was uncovered at the GATT Uruguay Round that the multinational corporations tend to restrict access to their technologies by imposing a number of restrictions, such as:

- Requirements that inputs and components be acquired from specified sources often located in the industrialized countries or enterprises which they control.
- Prohibitions on improvement of plant and machinery.
- Retaining the right to control the quality of goods produced.
- Restricting the acquiring party from undertaking further research or adaptation of the technology to local conditions.
- Prejudicing the use of personnel of the acquiring country.
- Unjustifiably fixing the prices of the products manufactured by the acquiring party.
- Restriction on the exports of the product by the acquiring party.
- Payment and other obligations after expiration of industrial property.

Special Treatment for Developing Countries

Chapter 6 of the TOT code states that taking into consideration the needs and problems of developing countries, particularly those of the least developed countries, the governments of developed countries, directly or through appropriate international organizations in order to facilitate and encourage the initiation and strengthening of the scientific and technological capabilities of developing countries, so as to assist and cooperate with them in their efforts to fulfill their economic and social objectives, should take adequate specific measures, inter alia, to:

- Facilitate developing countries' access to available information regarding the availability, description, location and, as far as possible, approximate cost of technologies which might help these countries to attain their economic and social development objectives.
- Give developing countries the freest and fullest possible access to technologies where transfer is not subject to private decisions.
- Facilitate access by developing countries, to the extent practicable, to technologies where transfer is subject to private decisions.
- Assist and cooperate with developing countries in the assessment and adoption of existing technologies and in the development of national technologies by facilitating access as far as possible to available scientific and industrial research data.
- Cooperate in the development of scientific and technological resources in developing countries, including the creation and growth of innovative capacities.
- Assist developing countries in strengthening their technological capacity, especially in the basic sectors of their national economy, through creation of and support for laboratories, experimental facilities and institutions for training and research.
- Cooperate with the establishment or strengthening of national, regional and/or international institutions, including technology transfer centres, to help developing countries develop and obtain the technology and skills required for the establishment, development and enhancement of their technological capabilities, including the design, construction and operation of plants.
- Encourage the adoption of research and development engineering and design to conditions and factor endowments prevailing in the developing countries.
- Cooperate in measures leading to greater utilization of the managerial, engineering, design and technical experience of the personnel and the institutions of developing countries in specific economic and other development projects undertaken at the bilateral and multilateral levels.
- Encourage the training of personnel from developing countries.

Also, in chapter 6.3 of this instrument, the governments of the developed countries have a duty to take measures in accordance with their national policies, law and regulations to encourage and to endeavour to give incentives to enterprises and institutions in their countries, either individually or together with enterprises and institutions, particularly those in developing countries, to make special efforts, inter alia, to:

1) Assist in the development of technological capabilities of the enterprises in developing countries, including special training required by recipients.

2) Undertake the development of technology appropriate to the needs of developing countries.

3) Undertake R&D activity in developing countries of interest to such countries, as well as improve cooperation between enterprises and scientific and technological institutions of developed and developing countries;

4) Assist in projects by enterprises and institutions in developing countries for the development and adoption of new and existing technologies suitable to the particular needs and conditions of developing countries.

Chapter 6.4 of the code concluded by suggesting that the special treatment accorded to developing countries should be responsive to their economic and social objectives vis-à-vis their retentive stages of economic and social development. An example of an inter-regional international instrument is the case between 66 African countries, Caribbean and Pacific States and the European Community. The convention took place in 1984 and is better known as the Lomé Convention. In providing for cooperation between the two groups of States with a view to promoting their economic, cultural and social development, the former group asked for preferential treatment. The convention covered numerous areas such as agriculture, industrial development, mining, transport, trade and culture. Both technical and financial cooperation were used at the convention.

To achieve the above and to administer other TOT codes, International Institutional Machinery was established. And, as we saw in Table 8, a number of developed countries set up investment guarantee schemes in order to provide incentives to the enterprises in their territories so that they could transfer technology to developing countries.

Case Study 8: The FIRA Panel – Canada vs. the U.S.

In the FIRA Panel case, the United States had questioned the use of local purchasing and manufacturing requirements under Canada's Foreign Investment Review Act (FIRA) (1973) as being trade-distortive and inconsistent with the national treatment standards and other GATT provisions. It was also argued that export requirements under that law constituted unwarranted governmental interference in commercial operations and raised questions about the dumping of products abroad, as well as about the "nullification and impairment" of previous trade commitments. In response, Canada denied any such effects, and argued, inter alia, that the law left it to investors to make specific undertakings in the investment screening process and that while such undertakings were legally enforceable, they were not specifically imposed by the law. In its decision, the FIRA Panel found that "undertakings to purchase goods of Canadian origin ... exclude the possibility of purchasing available imported products so that the latter are clearly treated less favourably than domestic products". This constituted discrimination in favour of domestic products in violation of the GATT national treatment standard (art. 111.4). The Panel found the element of choice on the part of investors in making such undertakings to be irrelevant, so long as there was governmental involvement in the preferential treatment of domestic products. However, the Panel did not find the export requirements to be outside its terms of reference, which had only mentioned the two other requirements.

But one particular decision of special importance to developing countries was the Panel's statement (in response to arguments made by Argentina as an interested party in the case) that, "in disputes involving less-developed contracting parties, full account should be taken of the special provisions in the General Agreement relating to these countries" (such as art. XV111.C). As has become well established under GATT, developing countries are allowed greater flexibility in the use of trade-restrictive measures for a variety of reasons, including balance-of-payments problems, and infant industry and development considerations.

Note that the Panel's report was adopted on 7 February 1984, and Canada's Foreign Investment Review Act was replaced by the Investment Act 1985.

What is GATT and what is the WTO?

The WTO came into existence in 1995. It was the successor of the GATT, which was established in the wake of the Second World War. GATT was the only multilateral body governing international trade from 1948 until the establishment of the WTO, and in the early years concentrated on reducing the tariff barriers of each member country. Then came the Kennedy Round, which brought a GATT Anti-Dumping Agreement and a section on development. However, the Tokyo Round was when the first major attempt was made to tackle trade barriers that did not take the form of tariffs. The last GATT Round was the Uruguay Round, which lasted from 1986 to 1994.

In the 47 years of its existence, GATT succeeded in reducing tariffs to low levels and helped to spur a very high rate of world trade growth during the 1950s and 1960s. In fact, the growth was around 8% per year on average and this trade growth outpaced production growth throughout the GATT era. This growth, combined with a series of economic recessions in the 1970s and early 1980s, drove governments all over the globe to devise other forms of protection for sectors facing increased foreign competition in their countries. In Europe and North America there were high unemployment rates and the constant closure of factories. As a result, the Western governments started seeking bilateral market-sharing arrangements with competitors and embarked on subsidies races in order to maintain their shares in agricultural trade. The loopholes in the multilateral system were exploited and efforts to liberalize agricultural trade were unsuccessful. Even the GATT dispute settlement system was not respected. These and many other factors convinced the members that a new form of multilateral organization was needed, and at the Uruguay Round the Marrakech Declaration resulted in the creation of the WTO.

In brief, the World Trade Organization (WTO) is the only international institution dealing with the global rules of trade between nations. Its main role is to ensure that trade and investment flows freely among its members. Using international instruments, the WTO fits five main areas together – goods, services, intellectual property, disputes and trade policy reviews. The first three – in the form of TRIPS, TRIMS and GATS – are directly relevant to developing countries' industrialization and we shall be looking at their role in the transfer of technology in particular.

International Instruments

The use of the word "instrument" here means the variety of forms and effects of the international acts and documents used in reaching agreements and resolutions. The United Nations has, though long after China had started the copying culture, recognized the need for technologies to be transferred from developed countries to developing nations. As a result, a number of international multilateral instruments (universal or quasi universal in their memberships) have been entered into through the UN Agencies, GATT (General Agreement on Tariffs and Trade) and currently the World Trade Organization (WTO). These multilateral instruments contain measures relating to the transfer of technology and capacity building from the developed countries to the developing countries. Other international instruments include the interregional (which involves two or more regions), regional (membership is limited to a particular group, defined geographically), and bilateral agreements. Technology transfer conditions contained in such instruments follow different approaches, though these depend on the objects and purposes of the instruments. A few have in-built mechanisms, others are in the form of international cooperation deals, which may require the intervention of an international organization, or are in the form of a special institutional set-up for the implementation of provisions, e.g. the Law of the Sea Convention, which deals specifically with marine technology and capacity-building in the management, exploration and exploitation of marine resources. Most of these multilateral instruments aim to promote access to technologies and the development of local capacities in the developing countries. Another example of this is the Montreal Protocol, which deals with environmental technology protection on substances that deplete the ozone layer. The capacity of the parties to fulfill their obligations to comply with the control measures set out in the protocol depends on the effective implementation of financial cooperation and the transfer of technology to developing countries. Further examples are the TRIPS Agreement, the TRIMS Agreement and the GATS Agreement, where specific references are made to the transfer of technology to developing countries.

The TRIPS Agreement (Agreement on Trade-Related Aspects of Intellectual Property Rights)

Although the TRIPS Agreement refers to technology in a broader sense, it establishes minimum standards for intellectual property rights. This Agreement protects the inventors of technologies, and achieves its aim through the use of Patent Offices in almost every nation of the globe. The Patent Offices' responsibilities include the granting of Intellectual Property Rights such as patents, copyright and trademarks. They also have administrative functions, such as examining and granting or rejecting patents, designs and trademarks, and maintaining the registers of intellectual property in each country.

The basic hypothesis of the proposals for a global TRIPS regime presented by the leading industrialized nations is that adequate levels of intellectual property protection are essential for trade liberalization and for the encouragement of foreign direct investment and technology flow. In particular, being the main sources of technological innovation and of investment and technology flow in the world economy, transnational corporations are naturally concerned about the legal protection of such technologies in the global marketplace, as indicated by the following statement issued on the TRIPS negotiations by the Executive Board of the International Chamber of Commerce:

World business reaffirms its view that the Uruguay Round negotiation should produce agreed GATT arrangements dealing with the trade aspect of intellectual property rights, designed to establish fundamental principles and to ensure adequate national and international protection and enforcement for those rights. Such protection is also an important factor in encouraging greater flows of foreign direct investment in developing countries and in stimulating technical transfer to these countries (UNCTC, 1990: 2).

At the meeting, they stipulated the following standards or measures for intellectual property protection:

(a) The patentability of all inventions, regardless of subject matter (and hence, the abolition of specific patent exclusions, such as exclusions on pharmaceuticals, therapeutic methods, plant and animal varieties and food products). Such protection must confer exclusive use and manufacturing and commercial rights for at least 20 years;

(b) Protection of trademarks, including service marks, well-known marks and geographical names, on the basis of use or registration, for no less than ten-year terms, with an indefinite number of renewals and excluding others from using the same or similar marks for the same or similar goods;

(c) Copyright protection for all forms of original expression, regardless of the medium (i.e. computer programs, literary, musical, dramatic and cinematographic works and works in other forms) and comprising exclusive commercial, distribution and reproduction rights for the life of the author plus 50 years (or for 25 years in the case of computer programs);

(d) Legal protection for any original layout design of semiconductor chips or integrated circuits, in the form of exclusive use, reproduction and commercial rights for at least ten years;

(e) Limitation of compulsory licensing to situations recognized in relevant international conventions, or for reasons of national emergency or violation of anti-trust or competition laws, such licensing to be non-exclusive and subject to payment of compensation at market value;

(f) Enforcement measures, including the imposition of civil and criminal penalties, to deter infringements of intellectual property rights and trade in infringing goods both internally and at national borders;

(g) The application of national treatment, most favoured nation treatment and transparency standards to intellectual property laws and regulations.

However, there are divided views on the extent to which intellectual property protection actually promotes technology transfer to the developing countries. This is because some of the foreign investors abuse the privileges by registering their patents in developing countries and not transferring the technologies as stated previously. But another school of thought claimed that intellectual property rights would encourage FDI into the developing countries. How does it do so, when, instead of increasing, the FDI is decreasing in the developing countries? For example, the share of developing countries in world FDI is small and has fallen from the 1990s peak to 40% in 1994, to less than 20% in 2000. So has this actually encouraged the transfer of technology to the developing countries? No, it has rather been an obstacle to the transfer of technology from the developed countries to the developing countries. Newly industrialized countries such as Japan, Taiwan and South Korea did not experience this. In fact, they were called "the counterfeit capitals" of the world when they were industrializing. In the Netherlands and England (while industrializing) manufacturers produced copies in response to popular demand for ceramics from China, although these products were adjusted to local markets. For example, a wooden handle had to be added to the silver cups because the silver handle was too hot while holding the cup. In America during the nineteenth century, goods from Europe were considered superior and as such, the manufacturers were copying these products. In both continents, copying and imitation had few negative connotations then. But today, reverse engineering, imitation and many strategies of innovation to develop technology are either outlawed or made more difficult by the patent and copyright protection mandated by TRIPS. The Patent Offices are being used by Europe and America as their watchdogs and to police small enterprises in the developing countries, which they think are copying their technologies. Patent Offices in developing countries should discourage dangerous copying such as in medicine, and encourage local inventors of good products rather than acting as the developed countries' watchdogs using the TRIPS instruments. Also, article 27 of the TRIPS Agreement states that a "patent shall be available and patent rights enjoyable without discrimination as to ... whether products are imported or locally produced". This means that the developing countries have no right to discriminate against patent rights even after the expiration of a reasonable amount of time. TRIPS should allow the governments of the developing countries to fix reasonable timeframes for honouring foreign patents. It is only by agreeing to a shorter period that import replacement can be achieved. Also, TRIPS should allow governments of the developing countries to make laws that can enable the copying of technology when the patent owner fails to produce locally within a given time. The case between Brazil and the US can be used to illustrate this point:

Case Study 9: Brazil – Abuse vs. Compulsory Licenses Law

Brazilian law contains an article (Article 68) that authorizes local licences when manufactured goods are not produced locally. If a foreign company has obtained a patent for a product or process in Brazil but does not establish local production within three years, the law authorizes the Brazilian government to license local producers to produce the good (the term here is "local working"). This is the "industrial policy" article, with applications far beyond pharmaceuticals. By spurring foreign firms to establish local production it contributes to a more developmental foreign investment regime. But it is arguably in violation of TRIPS, and has been strongly opposed by the US. The US brought a WTO panel dispute against Brazil in 2000. In June 2001 the two countries signed a communiqué announcing the withdrawal of the US challenge, but they also affirmed that the fundamental conflict over Article 68 remained unresolved (Wade, 2003).

The US, however, threatened that if the Brazilians used Article 68 to issue a compulsory licence for non-pharmaceutical products as part of their wider industrial policy, the WTO case would be restarted. You know what this means. Whoever has the power has the justice! Again, the cost of going to court could be too high for Brazil, and in addition, Brazil may face reprisals from the US and Europe. Above all, this is a warning to other developing countries that may wish to emulate Brazil's efforts. With all these obstacles, how can the developing countries, particularly Africans, achieve any meaningful industrial transformation?

On the other hand, an example of a multilateral instrument in the area of incentives to developing countries is also covered in the Agreement on Trade-Related Aspects of Intellectual Property Rights (IPR). Article 66.2 of the TRIPS states that developed countries "shall provide incentives to enterprises and institutions in their territories". As stated above, such incentives to enterprises in their territories may include things like Investment Guarantee Schemes, illustrated in Table 8. But how often the developed countries give incentives without attaching trade conditionality is something to be investigated.

The Agreement on Trade-Related Aspects of Intellectual Property Rights (TRIPS) started operation in 1994, just at the end of the GATT Uruguay Round. It covers the protection of trademarks, copyrights, industrial designs, data secrets and patents (on drugs, and electronic and mechanical devices, etc.), the main two being copyrights and patents. The developed countries are supposed to use patents and copyrights to transfer technology to the developing countries, but they are not free to the developing country. TRIPS raises the prices of patents to the consumers, who are mainly from the developing countries. The developed countries are the net producers of patentable knowledge while the developing countries are the net consumers. A typical example is the case of Mexico. In 1996 the Mexican domestic patents were only 389, while the foreign applications were a record 30,000. Other handicaps we have seen above include the state's refusals on compulsory licensing and the abuse of licensing by the foreign inventors. There have been a number of complaints made by the developing countries on these issues, but see how the WTO Doha Ministerial Declaration put it:

We take note of the work done by the Council for Trade-Related Aspects of Intellectual Property Rights pursuant to paragraph 11.1 of the Doha Decision on Implementation. Related Issues and Concerns and paragraph 1.h of the Decision adopted by the General Council on 1 August 2004, and direct it to continue its examination of the scope and modalities for complaints of the types provided for under sub-paragraphs 1(b) and 1(c) of article XXIII of GATT 1994 and make recommendations to our next session (WTO Doha Ministerial Meeting Instrument document).

The next session came and went, yet there was no conclusive agreement. Even during the 2009 G20 summit, little was mentioned about how to revive the failed trade talks.

In the TRIPS Agreement, it is clear that Intellectual Property Rights protection is tied up with the Special Treatment for Developing Countries in chapter 6 of the Code and article 66.2 of the TRIPS. Nowadays, almost all developing countries have Patent Offices in order to act as watchdogs for the developed countries' intellectual property, but instead of such protection leading to an increase in technology transfer, the technological gap is widening.

In the WTO Working Group Report of 2005, India, Pakistan and the Philippines highlighted the crucial things to be done by the developed countries, as follows:

1. They should take measures to encourage multinational firms to perform science and technology development work in host countries.
2. They should adopt practices that facilitate technology transfer and its rapid diffusion in the developing countries.
3. They should discourage the use of restrictive business practices by technology owners.

4. They should encourage the mobility of scientists, technologists and technicians under the GATS Agreement.

The above summarizes most of the things discussed in this chapter. Elaborating number 2 further, this book has already highlighted a lot of issues ranging from multinational corporations giving bribes, agricultural subsidies and a table of arguments relating to what Mr List called "kicking away the ladder". Obviously, the tackling of these issues by the developed countries would be enough incentive or encouragement for the least developed countries (LDC) to bridge the technological gap and develop also. But have they started or how much have the developed countries done so far? Article 66.2 mandated them as follows:

Developed country members shall provide incentives to enterprises and institutions in their territories for the purpose of promoting and encouraging technology transfer to least developed country members in order to enable them to create a sound and viable technological base.

To monitor the above mandate, the TRIPS Council mandated the developed countries to submit their country's self-report to the Council on the efforts they (individually) had made to increase incentives to enterprises and institutions in their territories, for the purpose of promoting and encouraging technology transfer to developing countries.

However, the TRIPS, in promulgating such mandates, made a number of lapses such as:

- It mentioned developed countries but failed to provide a list of those regarded as developed countries. That is, who is a developed country and who is not?
- It did not specify the type of incentives required that could amount to encouraging the transfer of technology. This could avoid the use of normal business transactions as a claim for incentives to LDC.
- It did not also ask the developed countries to state the volume and nature of the technology that had been transferred.

Nevertheless, the mandate to make this report to the TRIPS Council was initially ignored by the developed countries. It was only during the 1998 TRIPS Council meeting that a small country like Haiti requested further information from other WTO members regarding article 66.2 implementation, that some developed countries' self-reports started to appear to the Council. The 2001 WTO Doha Ministerial Conference again mandated that the TRIPS Council should design and put in place a monitoring mechanism for article 66.2. Then the Council obliged the developed countries not only to make three-yearly reports but to submit their self-reports covering 1999 to 2007 on incentives they had made to encourage the transfer of technology to developing countries. Since then, a number of developed countries have submitted their own reports to the TRIPS Council. The content of these reports provides material for a separate book, but before leaving this subject let us see how, in her analysis of developed countries' submissions to the TRIPS Council (1999–2007), Suerie Moon, a Doctorate Research Fellow at Harvard University, concludes:

The evidence arising from this review of country reports to the TRIPS Council does not paint a rosy picture of compliance with article 66.2. Lack of definitional clarity regarding the terms "technology transfer" and "developed country" make it unclear which countries are obligated to do what. Furthermore, many high-income and/or OECD countries have never submitted a report, and among countries that did, submissions have largely been irregular. In addition, a majority of the programmes and policies reported do not specifically target LDCs, let alone LDC WTO members. Furthermore, a significant proportion of programmes for LDCs do not actually target technology transfer. The country reports do describe a range of programmes that certainly may benefit LDCs. However, they do not provide sufficiently detailed data to determine whether article 66.2 led to any additional incentives beyond business as usual foreign aid (Moon, 2008).

The TRIMS Agreement (Agreement on Trade-Related Investment Measures)

This is another product of the Uruguay Round negotiation. It is a multilateral agreement seeking to establish multilateral standards to govern the use of trade-related investment measures by host countries. The idea of distortion has been the main focus of the discussion. Such distortion is considered to occur when business decisions are made by the home country on the basis of considerations other than market forces.

The main debate has been centred on two broad categories: performance requirements and investment incentives. Performance requirements are part of a much larger phenomenon, namely, measures to influence the location of production, the selection of inputs (e.g. local content requirement), the scale of operations and the marketing of outputs on the part of transnational corporations. Examples of investment incentives, meanwhile, are various forms of tax relief and exemptions, accelerated depreciation, import duty exemptions, subsidies, investment grants, priority access to credit, tariff protection and other forms of fiscal, financial and commercial inducements or protections for investments. In addition to these measures, two other categories of measures applied by transnational corporations and home countries have trade-distorting effects. Table 9 lists four categories of measures covered by TRIMS. These are performance requirements, investment incentives, corporate measures and home country measures. The possible effects on trade and investment flows can be summarized as follows:

Table 9: Trade-Related Investment Measures

Measures	Possible Economic Impact
Investment Incentives	Influence location of inventions
Tax concessions	
Tariff concessions	
Subsidies	
Investment grants	
Performance Requirements	
Local equity requirements	Restrict ownership of Investments
Licensing requirements	Require technology transfer
Remittance restrictions	Restrict external financial Transfers
Foreign exchange restrictions	Restrict external financial Transfers
Manufacturing limitations	Restrict production
Transfer of technology	Require technology transfer

Requirements	
Domestic sales requirements	Displace imports
Manufacturing requirements	Displace imports
Product mandating requirements	Displace other exports
Trade balancing requirements	Displace other exports
Local content requirements	Displace imports
Export requirements	Displace other exports
Import substitution requirements	Displace imports
Corporate measures (restrictive business practices)	
Market allocation	Restrict exports
Collusive tendering	Excessive pricing for imports
Refusal to deal	Restrict export/imports
Exclusive dealing	Export prohibition
Tied sales	Displace other import/exports
Resale price maintenance	Excessive pricing for imports
Price fixing	Excessive pricing
Differential pricing	Excessive pricing
Transfer pricing	Excessive pricing for imports and low pricing for exports
Home Country measures	
Export limitation on	Restrict trade

foreign affiliates	
Preferential taxes for income on inventions	Subsidize investments

Sources: UN Centre on Transnational Corporations, based on negotiating proposals at the Uruguay Round and other material

Let us describe some of these requirements in detail as follows:

1) Local equity requirements prescribe minimum percentages of local equity ownership, either as a general investment policy or in certain priority sectors, such as natural resource ventures in many developing countries. This mainly allows joint ventures between foreign and local investors in the particular country or sectors.

2) Technology transfer and licensing requirements are designed to ensure that foreign investors transfer or license particular types of technology to local firms or partners as a condition for conducting business in the host country.

3) Remittance and foreign exchange restrictions impose controls on the transfer of funds from the host country.

4) Manufacturing requirements oblige an investor to produce certain components or products locally and may be similar to local content requirements where the components are used as inputs in other manufacturing activities.

5) Manufacturing limitations prohibit a foreign investor from producing particular goods, which are often reserved for local firms.

6) Product mandating requirements are described in the Uruguay Round negotiations in terms similar to export requirements, in that a foreign investor is required to export particular products to specified countries or foreign markets.

7) Trade balancing requirements also overlap with export requirements in that they require investors to balance any imports by exporting a corresponding proportion or value of their own production.

8) Local content requirements prescribe the minimum percentage of domestic inputs in the manufacturing process, in order to ensure or promote the use of local products and fuller integration of foreign investments in the national economy. We saw a typical example of this in Chapter Five.

9) Investment incentives: host countries attempt to deal with structural imbalances in their economies by giving special advantages to investments, in particular sectors or locations. They can be in the form of fiscal, financial or commercial breaks, and can be found in virtually every country in the world.

10) Performance requirements are used to foster the integration of foreign affiliates into the national economy and to enhance their contributions to development objectives and to minimize perceived negative effects of global corporate strategies, such as intra-group transfers of income to profit centres outside the host country and corporate restrictions on transfer of technology and on the trading patterns of affiliates or licensees.

Having claimed the above impacts, the extent to which performance requirements and investment incentives bring benefits or cause economic distortions and inefficiencies is mixed – whether it actually alters trade patterns, attracts investors, displaces production or costs jobs tends to be overstated, although the impact may vary between industries. This is because the competition to attract foreign investments is seen to force countries to offer more incentives than they otherwise would, resulting in a degree of subsidization that nullifies or reduces gains from the investment. But the central criticism has been that any government measure that seeks to alter or influence investment decisions is an unwanted interference in the free operation of market forces and a distortion of the levels and patterns of trade and investment flows. This leads to negative consequences for the economic well-being of the countries concerned and for the efficient allocation of the world's resources. This should be the main concern of the WTO. But because investors are in short supply, investment incentives cannot be avoided and without performance requirements, foreign investments are bound to have negative effects on the host country.

During the time of GATT, developing countries were allowed to discriminate by using "Performance Requirements" such as "Local Content Requirements" and "Requirements to use local managers or suppliers". These could allow the developing countries to regulate the behaviours of the multinational corporations operating in their countries. But in the recent Doha Ministerial meetings of the WTO, the US and Europe pressed for a ban on all forms of performance requirements, including joint venturing, technology transfers and research and development. India and Brazil have fought hard to stop them from modifying the TRIMS Agreement. This and other issues show that there is considerable dispute, both among the developed countries and between them and the developing countries, on the characterization of particular measures of TRIMS.

The GATS Agreement (General Agreement on Trade in Services)

This agreement also came out of the Uruguay Round, and negotiation around it has intensified at the WTO since 2000. The negotiation is aimed at the establishment of a multilateral framework of principles and rules for trade in services, including everything from banking and education to rubbish collection, tourism, health service, water supply and sanitation. Work on such a framework is expected to lead to conditions of transparency and progressive liberalization, and will be a means of promoting the economic growth of all trading partners.

The task of drafting a services framework was given to the Group of Negotiations on Services, which was established separately from other negotiating groups. The initial work of the group centred on the following elements:

- Definitional and statistical issues;
- Broad concepts on which principles and rules for trade in services, including possible disciplines for individual industries, might be based;
- Coverage of the multilateral framework for trade in services;
- Existing international disciplines and arrangements; and
- Measures and practices contributing to or limiting the expansion of trade in services, including specifically any barriers perceived by individual participants, to which the conditions of transparency and progressive liberalization might be applicable.

While examining the possible implications and the applicability of concepts, principles and rules for particular industries and specific transactions, in 1989 the group tested the following industries: telecommunications; construction; transportation; tourism; professional and financial services; and insurance. These are industries where foreign direct investment is mostly required. Proposals were submitted by a number of countries and were merged with the report of the group. They were therefore included in the mid-term review declaration, which recognizes that the multilateral framework may include "trade in services involving cross-border movement of services, cross-border movement of consumers, and cross-border movement of factors of production where such movement is essential to suppliers".

WTO Report
The Working Group eventually completed its report in 2005, which is partly reproduced here.

WTO – Report (2005) of the Working Group on Trade and Transfer of Technology to the General Council

INTRODUCTION
The Working Group on Trade and Transfer of Technology was established at the Fourth Ministerial Conference in Doha in November 2001, with the following mandate:

"We agree to an examination, in a Working Group under the auspices of the General Council, of the relationship between trade and transfer of technology, and of any possible recommendations on steps that might be taken within the mandate of the WTO to increase flows of technology to developing countries. The General Council shall report to the Fifth Session of the Ministerial Conference on progress in the examination".

Since its report to the General Council in 2004, the Working Group has held three formal sessions on 11 April 2005, 6 July 2005 and 11 October 2005. The minutes of these meetings are contained in documents WT/WGTTT/M/11, WT/WGTTT/M/12 and WT/WGTTT/M/13 respectively. As in the previous year, members pursued the work by continuing the analysis of the relationship between trade and transfer of technology, as well as discussing any possible recommendations on steps that might be taken within the mandate of the WTO to increase flows of technology to developing countries.

RELATIONSHIP BETWEEN TRADE AND TRANSFER OF TECHNOLOGY
This issue was taken up at the Eleventh, Twelfth and Thirteenth Sessions of the Working Group. In addition to continuing discussions on some of the elements of the relationship between trade and transfer of technology highlighted in earlier submissions, the members benefited from the presentation of three useful studies by UNCTAD, namely: (i) Facilitat-

ing Transfer of Technology to Developing Countries: A Survey of Home Country Measures; (ii) A Case Study on the Electronics Industry in Thailand; and (iii) Taxation and Technology Transfer: Key Issues.

At the Eleventh Session, members engaged in a useful discussion on the study, "Facilitating Transfer of Technology to Developing Countries: A Survey of Home-Country Measures", which had been introduced by UNCTAD at the earlier session of the Working Group. The study provided a useful compilation of home-country measures and highlighted the important role that home-country measures could play in encouraging flows of technology to developing countries. The ensuing discussion underscored the importance of investment in research and the role that the transfer of technology to developing countries could play as a powerful tool for development. Underpinning the significance of a holistic approach to a better understanding of the interface between trade and transfer of technology, it was suggested that further studies on "host-country measures" and "domestic research and development programmes" that have been successful in generating industrial development and economic growth, could be useful in furthering the work of the Working Group. There was a broad acknowledgement that both the private and public sectors had an important role to play in technology transfer through cohesive partnerships.

At this session, UNCTAD also introduced "A Case Study on the Electronics Industry in Thailand", which highlighted the contribution of the manufacturing sector of Thailand to the country's rapid export growth in recent years. The study underlined the role of host-country measures in technology transfer by throwing light on some of the proactive policies pursued by the Government of Thailand. These policies, according to the study, played a crucial role in creating a favourable environment for export-oriented FDI, promotion of technology transfer, its diffusion, innovation in the industry and an enabling framework for the emergence of domestic support industries. These initiatives had played an important role in integrating domestic contract manufacturers into the global production networks of transnational corporations (TNCs) and in acquiring assembly process capabilities, enhancing export competitiveness, and building up domestic supplier networks in the electronics industry.

At the Twelfth Session, the group considered UNCTAD's study on "Taxation and Technology Transfer: Key Issues". The study raised a number of issues with regard to the implications of various tax instruments on the transfer of technology from the perspective of both technology importing and exporting countries. In identifying some of the tax-related policy instruments that could be used to promote technology transfer to developing countries, the study underlined the important role that tax policy could play in relation to flows of technology, both as an incentive to attract technology and as a stimulant to technology exports. The tax structure of a country was a determinant factor in the nature and flow of technology. The study showed that the challenge for the technology-importing countries was to balance the need to facilitate technology acquisition by providing tax incentives with the need to maximize revenue collection. Similarly, technology-exporting countries had to find a balance between the level of tax incentives that could be provided to encourage local firms to export technology, and the need to maximize tax revenue collection from income generated by the activities of these firms abroad. It also highlighted the mitigating effects of excessive corporate income tax, high import duties, excessive taxation of dividends, royalties and technical fees, and the high withholding of taxes on technology transfers. A clear vision of national development goals with prioritization of economic activities, coupled with carefully targeted tax incentives, was considered as playing an important role in investment decisions and efforts to acquire technology through trade and FDI flows. Consideration of these issues continued at the Thirteenth Session.

POSSIBLE RECOMMENDATIONS ON STEPS THAT MIGHT BE TAKEN WITHIN THE MANDATE OF THE WTO TO INCREASE FLOWS OF TECHNOLOGY TO DEVELOPING COUNTRIES

Members continued their consideration of any possible recommendations on steps that might be taken within the mandate of the WTO to increase flows of technology to developing countries based on a joint submission tabled by a group of developing countries. These submissions indicated a number of areas where the proponents felt that recommendations could be made by the Working Group of steps that could be taken to facilitate the transfer of technology to developing countries. Members have, thus far, undertaken some work on the first two recommendations, namely: (i) an examination of the different provisions contained in various WTO agreements relating to technology transfer; and (ii) the provisions contained in various WTO agreements, which may have the effect of hindering the transfer of technology to developing countries.

At the Eleventh Session, the Working Group was briefed on the work carried out by the Council for Trade in Services in the context of Articles IV and XXV of the GATS. Members were informed that the architecture of GATS tended to place many of the actual commitments undertaken by members in the sphere of negotiated bilateral commitments. It was also indicated that the Special Session of the Services Council had held discussions on operationalizing Article IV, mainly through the examination of the Category II S&D proposals referred to by the General Council in 2003. The issue of the transfer of technology had been raised in those discussions as well, in particular, in the context of Article IV:1.

At the Twelfth Session, members considered a communication from Cuba, which underscored the need to review the effectiveness of the provisions on technology transfer in the WTO agreements and to assess the extent to which those agreements hindered flows of technology to developing countries. The communication also stressed the need to make concrete recommendations, at least as regards the first two recommendations, to the Sixth Ministerial Conference. In that context, it was suggested that at the General Council meeting in July, members should approve decisions that could guide the work of the Working Group in the run-up to the Hong Kong Ministerial Conference. During the course of the discussion on Cuba's communication, some members thought that stepping up the work of the Working Group in the run-up to the Hong Kong Ministerial Conference was crucial to making progress on possible recommendations. Others felt that since the issue was complex and members' understanding of it was still superficial, it called into question the repeated demand for developing recommendations. In their view, members needed to fully explore all related aspects of the issue to develop a clear understanding of the nexus between trade and transfer of technology, before looking at possible recommendations.

In the Thirteenth Session, members engaged in a constructive discussion on a new submission by India, Pakistan and the Philippines, which highlighted the crucial role of technology and technical knowhow in improving productivity, promoting export growth and attaining developmental goals. The submission stressed that the possible recommendations which the Working Group make might, among others, include: steps to expand technical assistance under the TRIPS Agreement; measures to encourage and incentivize multinational firms in developed countries to perform science and technology development work in host countries; adoption of practices that facilitate technology transfer and its rapid diffusion in the developing countries; discouraging the use of restrictive business practices by technology owners; and ways of expanding or encouraging the mobility of scientists, technologists and technicians under the GATS Agreement.

A number of members thought that the submission was useful as it was focused on and contained pragmatic elements for possible recommendations that the Working Group could consider in the future. A few members again questioned the competence of the Working Group in addressing some of the issues raised in the submission. Those members felt that these issues should ideally be addressed in relevant WTO bodies, which were equipped with the necessary knowledge and expertise to do so. However, other members reiterated that the Working Group was the appropriate forum to discuss these issues because Ministers at Doha had mandated it to do so, and perhaps even more importantly, because transfer of technology was a cross-cutting issue which could only be considered in a holistic manner by a body which had a broad perspective.

FUTURE WORK

The Working Group on Trade and Transfer of Technology has proceeded with the examination of the relationship between trade and transfer of technology and has continued the consideration of any possible recommendations on steps that might be taken within the mandate of the WTO to increase flows of technology to developing countries. Discussions have taken place on a number of issues, including in the context of submissions by members and studies presented by other intergovernmental organizations. Although the work carried out in the Working Group has contributed to a better understanding of the issues involved, a lot of work still remains to be done. In view of the relevance of the relationship between trade and transfer of technology to the development dimension of the Doha Work Programme, members recommend that the Working Group should continue their work with a view to fulfilling the mandate contained in paragraph 37 of the Doha Ministerial Declaration.

Obviously, the adoption of technology-related provisions is an expression of governments' willingness to cooperate internationally to redress or reduce the asymmetric distribution of scientific and technological capabilities in the world. The developed countries' governments have been participating in these agreements to transfer their technology to developing countries because they believe that they have moral obligations to do so – where all people are seen to be brothers and sisters. If this is correct, a "tit-for-tat" or "reciprocity" mentality while negotiating with the developing countries is unnecessary. We know very well that the bargaining powers are

170

not equal – there are the strong players and the weak players. Remember that the fear of social instability caused by the unrestrained power of employers over employees drove the decisions of those early twentieth-century British judges to give trade unions legal privileges in order to force a degree of restraint on the part of employers. Similarly, to maintain universal social stability, the developed countries have to force a degree of restraint onto their organizations operating in developing countries, especially in terms of issues such as competition rules, bribery and corruption, and the abuse of human rights. Unless there is sincerity and committed intentions on the part of the strong players, the status quo will remain. That is why a remarkable gap still exists between the intentions expressed in the instruments and their effective implementation. This is because some of the provisions are not legally binding, some are voluntary, while others are hortatory and not mandatory in character. Besides, the parties are usually sovereign countries with sovereign immunity. So, the question is whether non-compliance with any provision of the instruments could give rise to complaints by the affected members under the WTO's Dispute Settlement Understanding. In theory yes, but in practice no. No, because the weak country that took matters to the WTO DSM would be bullied and sanctioned by the stronger players. What an equal world we live in!

The Five Misunderstandings in the WTO

1. Does the WTO dictate terms?

The WTO acts as a moderator of the meetings. The decisions taken at the WTO are negotiated but not necessarily democratic. But the WTO can have a direct impact on a government's policies if disputes between members are brought to its attention. They are the Dispute Settlement Body and therefore the Judge. This means the WTO decides at the Dispute Settlement Mechanism (DSM) when a government (usually from a developing country) has broken any of the rules agreed during WTO negotiations. In theory, the complainant (usually from the developed country) should provide evidence to show that a specific requirement is distorting, but in practice they do not. They simply assert that such requirements are distorting and, as dominant actors, their assertions usually prevail.

2. Is the WTO for free trade?

Yes, it is. It facilitates negotiations on trade liberalization. It also provides the rules for how liberalization can take place. However, in making its rules it takes into consideration such matters as "fair trade" – subsidies or dumping. It claims to know the problems that the developing countries are facing and therefore includes special provisions for them. But trade liberalization is not actually helping the developing countries. Liberalization encourages "dumping" of consumer goods from the developed countries to the developing countries' territories. Therefore, it does not encourage the survival of infant industries in the developing countries. As a result, employment opportunities are not enough to absorb the teeming populations in the developing countries.

3. Does the WTO encourage development?

The WTO assumes that trade liberalization can boost economic growth. As a result, its agreements include many provisions that specifically take developing countries' interests into account, such as "special treatment" for the least developed countries. But it ends there. It does not include any punishment for breaches of such "special treatment". In short, no developing country has taken any developed country to the DSM for not granting them "special treatment". Of course, the cost of taking them to the DSM would be too high for them, coupled with the threat of sanctions and intimidation. Also, with the dumping of developed countries' goods and the consequential killing of infant industries in the developing countries, the commercial interest of WTO members has taken priority over development.

4. Does the WTO wreck jobs in developing countries?

Although attempts to ban "performance requirements" by the US and Europe during the WTO 2001 Round failed, any attempt by any developing country to use it may receive a threat of sanctions from the big actors. This, and the dumping of consumer goods, definitely affects the development of infant industries, thereby affecting the prospect of job opportunities in the developing countries. Let's not fool ourselves: jobs are created in the countries where consumer goods are manufactured rather than where they are consumed.

5. Are the small countries able to negotiate?

The multilateral negotiating rounds are supposed to be better for the developing countries than the bilateral ones. But in the WTO, the opposite is the case. Developed countries make threats to take developing countries to the WTO dispute resolution process; developed countries make more use of TRIPS review procedures to press countries to enforce intellectual property rules; they make threats to withdraw aid and to support rival states in political disputes, they complain to ministers or heads of state about uncompromising or aggressive ambassadors to Geneva, or even offer bribes to those who will cooperate with them.

The General Agreement on Tariffs and Trade (GATT), established in 1948, ended after many rounds with limited success. The Code of Conduct on the Transfer of Technology to developing countries remains mere rhetoric. With the above questions and answers, can the World Trade Organization (WTO), which took over from GATT, succeed? Look at what WTO had to say during the Doha Ministerial Declaration in 2006:

We take note of the report transmitted by the General Council on the work undertaken and progress made in the examination of the relationship between trade and transfer of technology and on the consideration of any possible recommendations on steps that might be taken within the mandate of the WTO to increase flows of technology to developing countries. Recognizing the relevance of the relationship between trade and transfer of technology to the development dimension of the Doha Work Programme and building on the work carried out to date, we agree that this work shall continue on the basis of the mandate contained in paragraph 37 of the Doha Ministerial Declaration. We instruct the General Council to report further to our next Session.

On the other hand, let us look at what renowned political economy authors such as Robert Hunter Wade, who is a fellow of the Institute of Development Studies at the University of Sussex, have had to say on the proliferation of international instruments:

The world is currently experiencing a surge of international regulations aimed at limiting the development policy options of developing country governments. Often, the three big agreements to come out of the Uruguay Round are investment measures (TRIMS), trade in services (GATS), and intellectual property rights (TRIPS) – the first two limit the authority of developing country governments to constrain the choices of companies operating in their territory, while the third requires the governments to enforce rigorous property rights of foreign (generally Western) firms. Together, the agreements make comprehensively illegal many of the industrial policy instruments used in the successful East Asian developers to nurture their own industrial and technological capabilities, and are likely to lock in the position of Western countries at the top of the world hierarchy of wealth (Wade, 2003).

His work describes how the three agreements constitute a modern version of Friedrich List's "kicking away the ladder". It also outlines some needed changes in the way we think about development and in the role of multilateral organizations. Wade concludes that the practical prospects for change along multilateral organizations lines are slender and negligible.

As Friedrich List, writing about unwanted competition (by England and the Netherlands) in his "kicking away the ladder" in the 1840s, observed:

It is a very clever common device that when anyone has attained the summit of greatness, he kicks away the ladder by which he has climbed up, in order to deprive others of the means of climbing up after him ... Any nation which by means of protective duties and restrictions on navigation has raised her manufacturing power and her navigation to such a degree of development that no other nation can sustain free competition with her, can do nothing wiser than to throw away these ladders of her greatness, to preach to other nations the benefits of free trade, and to declare in penitent tones that she has hitherto wandered in the paths of error, and has now for the first time succeeded in discovering the truth (List, 1966 (1885): 368).

List saw the preaching to other nations of the benefits of free trade as a feature of the new world system to tip the playing field even more against the developing countries. Almost all the developed countries went through stages of protectionist policy. Germany was protectionist when it was trying to catch up with Britain, while Britain was protectionist when it was trying to catch up with the Netherlands. In short, as Mehdi Shafaeddin affirmed during the UN conference in 1998: "Despite the fact that the Industrial Revolution contributed to the rapid industrialization of Great Britain, its industrial sector benefited from trade protection and other forms of government intervention in the trade flow through the Navigation Act and by means of political power and even military power". He went further to add that Great Britain began its trade liberalization after over two centuries of protectionism, and that it has become an advocate of universal free trade on the basis of the perception that it would provide the country with export markets and access to raw materials. The US was protectionist when it was trying to catch up with Germany and Britain, while Japan was protectionist since the time it started its industrialization programme right up until the 1970s.

Perhaps the starkest example of developed countries kicking away the ladder by which they climbed up is the use of multilateral organizations to make intellectual property rights laws – patents and copyrights in particular. In the past, for Europe, America and Japan, imitation did not have a negative meaning. The study of technology by duplication was acceptable everywhere. "To copy", "to imitate" or "to model" was closely linked to craftsmanship, and special schools were set up in some countries for this purpose. But today the developing countries are prohibited from doing this.

Now that China's surging manufactured exports are hurting manufacturers in the developed countries, what is its next step? Really, the developing countries are not new to the rhetoric of the multilateral organizations, starting from the time of GATT. More than 80 instruments have been put in place; yet, the technological gaps keep widening. Lack of effective implementation of these instruments therefore lends credence to the wisdom of any developing countries intending to commence a copying culture.

CHAPTER SEVEN
The Chinese Copying Culture

Chinese Disruptions

As we have seen in the previous chapters, "industrialized" status is not attained simply by establishing the factory system. Social virtues, development of commerce and commercial institutions such as in transportation, communication, banking, education, health, wholesale and retail services, as well as government policy, are all integral parts of the system. These are the prerequisites for economic growth that could catapult a nation to industrialized status. China is still lagging behind in some segments of this synergy; hence, it is regarded as a developing country. Otherwise, any country with nuclear weapons and possibly rockets to the moon should not be regarded as a developing country.

However, the factory sector plays a pivotal role in the overall transformation of societies. It generates productive employment, manufactures basic necessities for improved living standards and satisfies the consumption needs of growing populations. In particular, because it can create more employment opportunities than all other parts put together, our emphasis is on the factory system.

In Chapter One we saw that China invented many of the earlier technologies such as gunpowder, paper-making, and iron and steel, but its technological advancement was disrupted due to a series of attacks, wars and unequal treaties with foreign powers. First, the Mongols conquered northern China. Then came the British East India Company, which began as a trading partner but used opium grown in India to pay for Chinese products (including tea and silk), which it shipped to Europe. When the Chinese government protested against the trade in opium because it was debilitating its subjects, the British government went to war in 1840. But because there were internal problems in China at that time, the Chinese government decided to make peace with the British government in 1842, and signed an unequal treaty. The treaty resulted in the British acquisition of Hong Kong as a base for trade. In 1857 the French launched the second opium war and China was defeated in 1864. With this defeat, Britain and

France were not only able to trade in opium, but also the bilateral instruments signed meant that ten Chinese ports had to be opened for the Western traders. Although China was not colonized, the treaties with American and European powers made it a subordinate trading partner. It placed the foreigners in more privileged and dominating positions, and that had a great impact on the pace of technological development in China.

The foreign traders were interested only in immediate profits rather than the future development of China's economy. The Americans and Europeans saw China as the source of primary products for their home industries as well as a market for their cheap machine-made goods; however, tea exports were hit by the new tea plantations in India and silk was hit by Japanese competition. This affected the Chinese income and consequently led to the shift of new lines of export. The new line of products meant the adaptation of foreign goods using imported machines. From the 1860s the Chinese government introduced modern factory machines. Chinese entrepreneurs also supported the idea and started importing Western manufacturing technologies, but not sufficient to initiate a process of industrialization at the time. In 1895 Japan defeated China and a treaty was signed that allowed foreigners to legally set up foreign-owned industries in China. This opened up the country for foreign capital, which found its way into industrial production. In particular, due to the abundance of labour in China, wages were low and this attracted more investors into the country. The new industries owned by foreigners did not target the Chinese market alone. China was seen as a production base for exports within the Asian region. Meanwhile, the Chinese were able to acquire new skills, but management posts were initially held by the foreigners. Again, Chinese businessmen tried to emulate the foreigners, and started importing machinery from the West and setting up factories. Through their banking system, they were able to mobilize capital with which they started operations, but this capital was also coming from abroad, and as such, the whole exercise remained problematic because foreigners continued to exploit them and held back their technological development. This resulted in the emergence of a nationalist movement.

The Movement for National Goods

By the early twentieth century, Sun Yat Sen inspired the nationalist movement, which grew in response to foreign intervention and control of the economy. The nationalist elites waged economic war against foreign powers. Tariffs on imports were not seen as a good weapon initially; rather, they decided to promote national goods by denouncing the use of foreign goods as "unpatriotic". In other words, they called on the Chinese people to buy Chinese products so as to substitute foreign imports with locally produced goods. While the promotion of local products by the nationalist movement and government was occurring, schools were set up for the purpose of copying foreign products. Zheng Guanying, a social and economic reformer who lived between 1842 and 1922, told the people that they should buy machinery and produce cloth, felt, wool, yarn, velvet, foreign shirts and trousers, foreign socks, foreign umbrellas and other goods. "We should make glass, implements and fine copper, copy foreign watches, all absolutely similar, but better and cheaper in order to compete with all those necessities," he said. Call it "imitation" or "replication" or "copying", this model was at the heart of Zheng Guanying's strategy of trade war against the West. Even Chen Chi, who succeeded him, stated: "We must use machinery in order to copy foreign goods, only then can we recover our economic rights".

As for heavy industries such as fertilizer production, the adoption of the Soviet model and Soviet assistance to China made it inevitable that some large Soviet industries would have to be obtained from them. The Soviet aid had ceased by the end of 1960, but by then the Chinese had been able to establish a heavy industry base. Then, emphasis shifted to acquiring light industries that would manufacture consumer goods. They had to use credit facilities from foreign commercial banks in order to buy the technologies necessary for their industrialization programme, and the leaders realized that such credits would lead them into heavy indebtedness to the foreign banks and consequently, political dependence. Further consequences would include the loss of their sovereignty to the hands of foreigners. The government then considered foreign designs of products which could be copied patriotically in China. "People must be encouraged to copy foreign goods as superior imitations," a senior government official said. A movement for national goods emerged. After the collapse of the Qing government in 1912, the movement for national goods spread by public meetings, public speeches and the publication of specialized journals like National Goods Monthly.

Hundreds of thousands of propaganda items were distributed between 1912 and 1915. Handbills, advertisements, speeches, lectures, rallies, boycotts, exhibits and even museums were dedicated to publicizing the notion that it was the responsibility of every citizen to buy "national products". Goods were branded as either "Chinese" or "foreign".

The catalogues of the exhibitions listed the contents of every exhibition hall to guide visitors and provide detailed information for those who could not attend the exhibitions personally. To encourage copying or improvements in production, there were guides on manufacturing and management procedures, which gave local producers detailed instructions on mistakes to be avoided when imitating foreign imports. This obviously undermined patent and copyright rules and regulations. But in China, who cared about the rules and regulations on intellectual property when the government was actually encouraging their breach? Without this flagrant disregard of intellectual property rights, how can any developing country industrialize?

The "National Goods Movement" was not just the state's issue but everyone's obligation. Even ordinary people forced their local industries to manufacture more affordable copies of coveted imports. Unfortunately, some of the goods were frequently discarded when judged to be inferior in quality. This led to some producers going bankrupt because their products failed to compete with imports and were seen to be inferior by consumers. But a majority of the producers who were determined to make their fortunes out of the movement did indeed produce superior quality goods. In addition to the national goods movement, the government in July 1927 introduced a new tax on luxury goods and a one hundred percent increase in the customs tax on all imported commodities.

Although more consumers preferred the cheaper goods produced locally, some elites were keen to embrace foreign goods in order to differentiate themselves from the masses. This led to a two-tier economy, with the wealthy people turning towards specialized shops that sold European goods. Sometimes, copy culture succeeded in fooling them into mistaking the copy for the genuine article. To achieve the objectives of the national movement, it was agreed that the dissemination of information about design, production, retailing and marketing to the people, local associations and government institutions was necessary. Seminars were held during each exhibition to inform and educate merchants and ordinary visitors about the products on display. Commercial information was also spread in newspapers, textbooks, magazines and posters. During National Products Movement Week, which took place in July 1928, fliers were scattered from aeroplanes, slogans posted throughout the city, speeches given and articles written by prominent local politicians, and entrepreneurs as well as cinema and radio stations participated in the movement. Prior to the Movement Week, the Ministry of Industry and Commerce asked each province and every city to promote national goods by establishing a museum for these in their area.

Having achieved the objectives of the nationalist movement, the integration of China into the world market became the next target. The government started looking for a closer relationship with foreign governments. Efforts were made to establish links between Chinese producers and foreign trading partners. Every source of credit and assistance was pursued via the United Nations, and sometimes through consulting firms, and, at the same time, foreign investments were encouraged, with four special economic zones being set up. From the start of the international market, the products from Europe and America dominated the world. But in the 1930s China increasingly started exporting to the poor countries of the world. Today, China is not only exporting to the developing countries, but is reclaiming a growing part of international commerce and exporting its consumer goods to Europe and America. A nationalist movement of import substitution industrialization led to the copy culture, transformation of foreign products into national goods, and ultimately to what is now a formidable player in the global marketplace. China, a country that has been keen to create employment opportunities for its people through import substitution industrialization, has now moved to an export-led industrialization programme.

With export-led industrialization in mind, at the G20 summit held in London in 2009, China bought itself a bigger role in world politics. Its contribution to the International Monetary Fund (IMF) was particularly significant. This means a larger stake in international bodies, as it will give China a high voting share and voice in the IMF. Although such funding will help to maintain global financial stability, it will particularly boost China's export trade to the rest of the world. "The world is a marketplace," my grandmother told me.

Ahn, C.Y. (1991) "Technology Transfer and Economic Development: The Case of South Korea", in K. Minden (ed.) *Pacific Cooperation in Science and Technology*, Honolulu: East-West Center

Aikman, D. (1986) *The Pacific Rim: Area of Change, Area of Opportunity*, Boston: Little, Brown

Ajayi, J.F.A. and Crowder, M. (eds). (1971) *History of West Africa, Volume 1*, London: Longman

Al-Hassan, A.Y. and Hill, D.R. (1986) *Islamic Technology: An Illustrated History*, Paris: UNESCO, and Cambridge University Press

Ali, A. (1984) *The Need for Technical Skills and Innovative Capacity: The Case of Manufacturing Industries in Malaysia,*

Ali, A. (1992) *Malaysia's Industrialization, the Quest for Technology*, Oxford

Aliyu, A. (1995) *Industrialization in Nigeria – An Appraisal*

Allen, G. (1981) "Industrial policy and Innovation in Japan", in C. Carter (ed). *Industrial Policy and Innovation*, London: Heinemann

Balassa, B. et al (1971) *The Structure of Protection in Developing Countries*, Baltimore: Johns Hopkins University Press

Balassa, B. et al (1982) *Development Strategies in Semi-industrial Economies*, Baltimore: The Johns Hopkins University Press (for World Bank)

Banfield, E.C. (1958) *The Moral Basis of Backward Society*, Glencoe, Ill: Free Press

Batchelor, R.A., Major, R.L. and Morgan, A.D. (1980) *Industrialization and the Basis for Trade*, Cambridge: Cambridge University Press

Bellah, R.N. (1965) *Religion and Progress in Modern Asia*, Glencoe, Ill: Free Press

Bendix, R. (1967) "The Protestant Ethic – Revisited", *Comparative Studies in Society and History*

Berger, B. (ed.) (1991) *The Culture of Entrepreneurship*, San Francisco: Institute for Contemporary Studies

Berger, P.L. (1990) *The Capital Spirit: Toward a Religious Ethic of Wealth Creation*, San Francisco: Institute for Contemporary Studies

Berger, PL. and Hsiao, H-H.M. (1988) *In Search of An East Asian Development Model*, New Brunswick, N.J.: Transaction Books

Bhagwati, J. (1966) *The Economics of Underdeveloped Countries*, New York: McGraw-Hill

Biggs, T. (1988) "Financing the emergence of small and medium enterprises in Taiwan", *EEPA Discussion Paper 16*, Harvard Institute of International Development

Blau, P. (1964) *Exchange and Power in Social Life*, New York: Wiley

Blakeney, M. (1989) *Legal Aspects of the Transfer of Technology to Developing Countries*

Blim, M.L. (1990) *Made in Italy: Small-Scale Industrialization and its Consequences*, New York: Praeger

Blomstrom, M., Kravis, I. and Lipsey, R. (1988) *Multinational Firms and Manufactured Corporations*, New York:

Bollen, K. (1980) "Issues in the Comparative Management of Political Democracy", *American Sociological Review* 45, 370–90

Bond, M.H. and Hofstede, G. (1989) "The Cash Value of Confucian Values", *Human Systems Management,*

Bradford, C. (1986) "East Asian 'Model': Myths and Lessons," in J. Lewis and V. Kallab (eds.) *Development Strategies Reconsidered*, New Brunswick: Transaction Books

Brusco, S. and Righi, E. (1965) *Local Government Industrial Policy,*

Bryce, M. *Policies and Methods of Industrial Development*, New York: McGraw-Hill

Burgelman, R.A. and Maidique, M.A. (1988) *Strategic Management of Technology and Innovation*, Homewood, Illinois: R.D. Irwin, Inc.

Burton, J. (1983) "Picking Losers...? The Political Economy of Industrial Policy", *Hobart Paper*, London: Institute of Economic Affairs

Cary, L. (1998) *Guide to Raising Capital for Smaller Business*

Casey, B. (1991) *Recent Developments in West Germany's Apprenticeship Training System*, London: Policy Studies Institute

Chacko, G.K. (1986) "International Technology Transfer for Improved Production Functions", *Engineering Costs and Production Economics*

Chan, Y.H. (1990) "Industrialization and Technology Capability Development: A Critical Review of Industrialization and Industrial Technology Capability Development in Malaysia, *M.Sc Dissertation*, University of Sussex

Bibliography

Chandler, A.D. (1980) "Industrial Revolution and Institutional Arrangements", *Bulletin of American Academy of Arts and Sciences* 33, May: 33–50

Chandler, A.D. (1990) *Scale and Scope: The Dynamics of Industrial Capitalism*, Cambridge: Harvard University Press/Belknap

Chataway, J. and Allen, T. (2000) *Industrialization and Development: Prospects and Dilemmas*

Chaudhuri, S., "Technological Innovation in a Research Laboratory in India: A Case Study", *Research Policy*

Chee, P.L. (1990) *International Capital Flows and Economic Development in Asia-Pacific Region*

Chen, E.K.Y. and Wong, T. "The Future Direction of Industrial Development in the Asian Newly Industrialised Economies", in S. Jang-Won (ed.) *Strategies for Industrial Development: Concept and Policy Issues*, Kuala Lumpur: Asian and Pacific Development Centre and Korea Development Institute

Chng, M.K., Low, Linda, Nga, T.B. and Tyabji, A. (1986) *Technology and Skill in Singapore*, Singapore: Institute of Southeast Asian Studies

Chou, J. (1987) "Economic Evaluation of Investment Incentive Scheme from a Macro Standpoint", *Research Report*, Tapei: Chung-hua Institution for Economic Research (Chinese)

Church, J. (1996) "War Against Sleaze", *Time Magazine*, 6 May

Clegg, S.R. and Redding, S.G. (1990) *Capitalism in Contrasting Cultures*, Berlin: Walter de Gruyter

Coleman, J. Social Capital 1990 (critical perspectives)

Comisso, E. and Tyson, L. (eds.) (1986) *Power Purpose and Collective Choice: Economic Strategies in Socialist States*, Ithaca: Cornell University Press

Commonwealth Secretariat (1985) "Technology Change: Enhancing the Benefits", *Report of a Commonwealth Working Group*, Vol. 1, London

Copeland, L (1986) "Skills Transfer and Training Overseas", *Personnel Administrator*

Corbo, V. and de Melo, J. (1987) "Lessons from the Southern Cone Policy Reforms", *World Bank Research Observer*, 2(2): 111–42

Corden, M. (1974) *Trade Policy and Economic Welfare*, London: Oxford University Press

Cropsey, J. (1955) "What is Welfare Economics?", *Ethics*

Dahlman, C.J. and Ross-Larson, B. (1987) "Managing Technological Development: Lessons from the Newly Industrializing Countries", *World Development*

Darwin, C. (1859) ed. By J.W. Burrow 1968 The Origin of Species, Penguin Book, London. This is a reprinting of Darwin 1859.

Davidow, William H. and Malone (1992) *The Virtual Corporation: Structuring and Revitalizing the Corporation for the 21st Century* place and publisher

Debresson, C.J. (1989) "Breeding Innovation Clusters: A Source of Dynamic Development", *World Development*

Department for International Development (DFID) (2006) "Making Governance Work for the Poor"

Deyo, F. (1987) "Coalitions, Institutions and Linkage Sequencing", in F. Deyo (ed.) *The Political Economy of the New Asian Industrialization*, Ithaca: Cornell University Press

Dikotter, F. (2007) *Things Modern – Material Culture and Everyday Life in China*

Dilke, C. (1867) *Greater Britain*

Djang, T.K. (1977) "Industry and Labor in Taiwan", *Monograph Series No. 10*, Institute of Economics, Academia Sinica, Taipei

Dunlop, J., Harbison, F. et al (1975) *Industrialism Reconsidered: Some Perspectives on a Study over Two Decades of the Problems of Labour*, Princeton Inter-University Study for Human Resources

Dyer, W.G. (1986) *Cultural Change in Family Firms: Anticipating and Managing Business and Family Transitions*, San Francisco: Jossey-Bass Publishers

Eckstein, H. (1990) "Political Culture and Political Change", *American Political Science Review*

Eisenstadt, S.N. (ed.) (1968) *The Protestant Ethic and Modernization: A Comparative View*, New York: Basic Books

Ekeh, L.U. (1993) "Technology Transfer and Nigeria Industrialization", *M.A. Dissertation*, University of Westminster, London

Engels, F. Conditions of Working-Class in England, 1844

Euromoney Publication, "International Privatisation Review 1998/99"

Fallows, J. (1994) *Looking at the Sun: The Rise of the New East Asian Economic and Political System*, New York: Pantheon Books

Feuerwerker, A. (1970) *China's Early Industrialization*, Cambridge, Mass: Harvard University Press, 1958, reprinted New York: Atheneum

Bibliography

Fichte (1806) "To the German Nation" by A German philosophy and reformer

Fisher, W.A. (1979) *Institutional Development of Appropriate Industrial Technology in Developing Countries*

Foster, D. (1980) *Innovation and Employment*, Oxford: Pergamon Press

Fukuyama, F. (1995) *Trust: The Social Virtues and the Creation of Prosperity*

Garofoli, G. (1992) *Endogenous Development and Southern Europe*

Gereffi et al (1994) Beyond the Producer-driven / Buyer-driven Dichotomy

Gimpel, J. (1977) *The Medieval Machine: The Industrial Revolution of the Middle Ages*, London: Gollancz

Goonatilake, S. (1984) *Aborted Discovery: Science and Creativity in the Third World*, London: Zed Books

Headrick, D.R. (1981) *The Tools of Empire: Technology and European Imperialism in the Nineteenth Century*, New York: Oxford University Press

Hobson, J. (1894) *Evolution of Modern Capitalism*

Howard, M. (2007) *Empires, Nations and Wars*,

Huberman, L. (1968) *Man's Worldly Goods: The Story of the Wealth of Nations*

Institute of Development Studies (1999)   Working Paper 100

Kang, H.-C. (1986) *Promotion of Technology Utilization in Selected Asian Countries: A Report*, Bangalore: Asian and Pacific Centre for Transfer of Technology

Kemp, T. (1989) *Industrialization in the Non-Western World*

Kitching (1989) Development and Underdevelopment in Historical Perspective

Klitgaard, R., Gray, W.C., Kaufmann, D. and Paolo, M. (1998) Fighting Corruption Worldwide, *Finance & Development Magazine*, March

Konczacki, Z.A. and Konczacki, J.M. (eds.) (1977) *An Economic History of Tropical Africa*, London: Cass

Lasserre, P. and Schutte, H. (date), *Strategies for Asia Pacific*

Lim, D. (1975) "Industrialization and Unemployment in West Malaysia", in D. Lim (ed.) *Readings on Malaysian Economic Development,* Kuala Lumpur: Oxford University Press

List F. (1966) (1885) The National System of Political Economy, New York: Augustus Kelley

Marton, K. (1986) "Technology Transfer to Developing Countries Via Multinationals", *World Economy*

Marx, K. Capital: a critique of political economy, ed. By Ernest Mandel, David Fernbach (1991)

Montagnon, P. (1990) "Export Control Likely for Third World", *Financial Times*, 30 August, London

Moon, S. (2008) "Does TRIPS Art. 66.2 Encourage Technology Transfer to LDCs? An Analysis of Country Submissions to the TRIPS Council (1999-2007)", *Policy Brief No. 2, UNCTAD*

Nurul, I. (1988) *Economic Independence between Rich and Poor Nations*

Oliver, R. and Fage, J.D. (1970) *A Short History of Africa*, 3rd edition, Harmondsworth: Penguin

Pacey, A. (2001) *Technology in World Civilization*

Parry, T.G. (1988) "The Multinational Enterprise and Restrictive Conditions in International Technology Transfer: Some New Australian Evidence", *Journal of Industrial Economics*

Patvardhan, V.S. (1990) Growth of Indigenous Entrepreneurship

Peel, M. (2009) "Lawyer's case will test powers of extradition", *Financial Times*, 1 June

Perlmutter, H. and Sagafi-Nejad, T. (1981) The UN and Transnational Corporations

Pyke, F. and Sengenberger, W (eds.) (date) *Industrial District and Local Economic Regeneration: Research and Policy Issues*

Qaisar, A.J. (1982) *The Indian Response to European Technology and Culture, 1498–1707*, Delhi: Oxford University Press

Bibliography

Raffer K. And H. W. Singer (2001) The Economic North-South Divide: Six Decades of Unequal Development

Reddie, R.S. (2007) *Abolition, Lion*, Oxford:

Roberts, J.M. (1994) *An Illustrated History of the World*

Rodney, W. (1973) *How Europe Underdeveloped Africa*

Sauvain, P. (1996) *British Economic and Social History: 1700–1870*

Schmitz, H. and Knorringa, P. (1999) "Learning from Global Buyers", *IDS Working Papers*

Smith, A. (2007), ed. By Eamonn Butler *The Theory of Moral Sentiments*

The Independent Newspaper (2005) "The Africa Issue", 1 June

UNCTC (1990) "New Issues in the Uruguay Round of Multilateral Trade Negotiations", UN SA 19

Unctad (2001) *Compendium on Transfer of Technology Instruments*

UNIDO (1990) "Identification, Formulation, Implementation and Monitoring of Multinational Industrial Enterprises"

UNIDO (1991) "Malaysia, Sustaining the Industrial Investment Momentum"

UNIDO Secretariat "A Strategy of Industrial Development for the Small, Resource Poor, Least Developed Countries"

van Dijk, P.M. (date) *The Interrelations between Industrial Districts and Technological Capabilities Development: Concepts and Issues"*

Wade, R.H. (1990) *Governing the Market – Economic Theory and the Role of Government in East Asian Industrialisation*

Wade, R.H. (2003)"What Strategies are Viable for Developing Countries Today? The WTO and the Shrinking of Development Space?" *Review of International Political Economy*, 4 November

Wallace, L. (1997) "Deepening Structural Reform in Africa: Lessons from East Asia", Tadahiko Makagawa, IMF: 81–83

White, L. (1962) *Medieval Technology and Social Change*, Oxford: Oxford University Press

Wilson, D. and Game, C. (2002) *Local Government in the United Kingdom*

Worsley, P. (1984) *The Three Worlds: Culture and World Development,* London: Weidenfeld and Nicolson

WTO Doha Ministerial Meeting Instrument document

INDEX

A

abuses 3, 123, 126, 147, 157-8, 171,
   191
AD 7-8, 11, 13-15, 22, 29, 191
ADB (Asian Development Bank)
   98, 100, 191
Administrative Order *see* AO
adoption 54, 129, 145, 147, 149-50,
   169-70, 179, 191
Africa 8, 11-12, 24, 26-8, 30, 54, 56,
   71-3, 117, 124-5, 187, 191
African countries 1, 11, 42, 56, 150
agreements
  franchise 125, 195
  technological 124
Agricultural Resources 89
Agricultural Resources Industrial
   191
agricultural subsidies 3, 30, 39, 44,
   72, 77, 82, 159, 191
Ali 144, 183, 191
Aliyu 80-1, 183, 191
ambassadors 20-1, 191
Amended BOT Law 107, 191
America 24, 28, 37, 40, 43, 156,
   175, 181, 191
ANAMCO 87, 191
ancillary industries 48, 80-1, 191
  efficient 143
AO (Administrative Order) 107, 191
application of national treatment
   129, 155, 191
Appropriate Industrial Technology in
   Developing Countries 187
Arab investors 39, 191
Asia 8, 14, 17, 102, 117, 125, 185,
   189, 191
Asian and Pacific Centre for Transfer
   of Technology 187, 191
Asian countries 82, 103
Asian Development Bank *see* ADB
Asian Industrialization 202

Asian Newly Industrialized 191
Asian Tigers 1-2, 33, 191
assistance 46, 56, 98-9, 115, 133,
   181, 191
audit 60, 191-2
audit committee 67
automation 140-1, 191, 197

B

backward, technologica lly 131
balance, favourable 6
Balassa 183, 191
Baltimore 183, 191
barriers, non-tariff 77, 200
BC 8, 13-14
Belgium 136, 191
Benin 71, 76, 191
Berger 183, 191
bonds 112, 184, 191
BOOT (Build-Own-Operate-
   Transfer) 107, 191-2
borrower 27, 78, 101-2, 191
BOT (Build-Operate-and-Transfer)
   106-9, 191-2
BOT Centre 107-9, 191
BOT Law 107, 191
Brazil 47, 52, 70, 74, 76, 94, 156-7,
   164, 192
bribery 27, 41, 50, 52-3, 55, 171,
   192
bribes 50-3, 55, 159, 173, 192
Britain 18, 25, 37, 55, 59, 78, 174,
   178, 186, 192
British banks 73-4
British call Industrial Estates 45
British Local Government System
   59, 192
BTPT (Build-Today-and-Privatize-
   Tomorrow) 2, 102-3, 192
BTPT building industries 192
Build-Operate-and-Transfer *see* BOT
Build-Own-Operate-Transfer
   (BOOT) 107, 191-2
Build-Today-and-Privatize-
   Tomorrow *see* BTPT